Robert Forman Horton

Inspiration and the Bible

An Inquiry. Fourth Edition

Robert Forman Horton

Inspiration and the Bible
An Inquiry. Fourth Edition

ISBN/EAN: 9783337183325

Printed in Europe, USA, Canada, Australia, Japan

Cover: Foto ©Lupo / pixelio.de

More available books at **www.hansebooks.com**

INSPIRATION AND THE BIBLE.

INSPIRATION AND THE BIBLE

AN INQUIRY

BY

ROBERT F. HORTON, M.A.

Late Fellow of New College, Oxford

FOURTH EDITION

London

T. FISHER UNWIN

26 PATERNOSTER SQUARE

MDCCCLXXXIX

"The only question concerning the truth of Christianity is, whether it be a real revelation, not whether it be attended with every circumstance which we should have looked for; *and concerning the authority of Scripture, whether it be what it claims to be, not whether it be a book of such sort, and so promulgated, as weak men are apt to fancy a book containing a Divine revelation should.* And therefore neither obscurity, nor seeming inaccuracy of style, nor various readings, nor early disputes, about the authors of particular parts; nor any other things of the like kind, though they had been much more considerable in degree than they are, could overthrow the authority of the Scripture; unless the prophets, apostles, or our Lord had promised that the book containing the Divine revelation should be secure from those things."

BUTLER: *Analogy*, part ii. ch. iii.

PREFACE TO THE SECOND EDITION.

I must ask my readers to remember that this is only an inquiry. If they assume it is anything more they must inevitably be disappointed. Some of my critics have complained that the work is destructive; the constructive element in it is given rather in the way of hint and suggestion than in a final and satisfactory form; of this fault I am painfully conscious. But to me, at any rate, the work of destruction is only a step to better and more permanent construction. Where narrow and partial views of Inspiration prevail, it is impossible to shape that nobler conception and doctrine of Inspiration for which the Church is at present waiting.

In the midst of many severe, and some unjust, attacks upon my work I have had abundant evidence, for which I humbly thank God, that "Inspiration and the Bible" has helped some inquiring spirits to make the difficult step from a traditional dogmatism into a position of greater strength and security; and with the fervent prayer that others may be helped, I issue a Second Edition.

If God grant me life and strength and opportunity, it is my great desire to issue a companion volume, "Revelation and the Bible," in which I shall try to review, sum up and estimate, those incalculable treasures of spiritual truth and practical help which have been stored up for our use by our Gracious God in the Inspired Book.

Should some other hand, abler than mine, be led to forestall me in this attempt, none will rejoice with a more genuine joy than the author of the present little book.

ROBERT F. HORTON.

October, 1888.

PREFACE TO THE FIRST EDITION.

MAY I bespeak the patience of two sorts of readers who may possibly look into this little book? Those who are acquainted with the movements of modern Biblical Scholarship will be disposed to say that all my facts are familiar, and all my conclusions are obvious. On the other hand, those who have not turned their minds to the important work which has recently been done in Biblical Scholarship, but who love their Bible dearly and reverence it profoundly, may be inclined to exclaim that in the facts pointed out and in the method of considering the facts there is something dangerous and subversive.

But it is the wide chasm between Biblical Scholarship on the one side, and what may be called the general way of regarding the Bible on the other side, that constitutes a serious danger at the present time. This little book could wish to be a small contribution towards a firm bridge across the chasm.

Those of us who love and reverence our Bible have fallen into a careless way of speaking about it, which is singularly misleading to those whose love and reverence for it are by no means established. Speaking of it as "The Word of God," we leave an impression that every text in it is a direct utterance of God; so that to question the accuracy of any statement in it seems like blasphemy, like charging God with a lie. Such impressions we do not give consciously or deliberately, and they are not the result of any careful study of the Book as a whole. But the indifferent or antagonistic, of whom there are very many, catch at our implied assertion. "This, you tell us," so they exclaim, "is the Word of God—very well; then are we to suppose that God wrote such passages as the three verses, Exodus iv. 24–26? And again, here are parts of the Book independent of one another and containing irreconcileable details. Are these contradictions chargeable on God?" Out of this admission, then, which we have so eagerly made, is manufactured the strongest weapon of the modern infidel. I hardly know an argument waged at the present day on the Secularist platforms which does not derive all its cogency from the false impression which we have ourselves given about the nature and claims of the Bible.

Now from this unfortunate error—an error which actually springs from our earnest and well-founded reverence for the Book—the researches of modern scholarship have, I believe, come to deliver us. That these researches are partly in the hands of avowedly rationalistic theologians need not terrify us; we do not refuse to build a church because the masons employed are freethinkers. I would venture to appropriate the results of present-day Biblical work in the interests of a believing theology. The rationalism, except so far as it means *reason*, can be left out of the question as the idiosyncracy of those minds to which on other accounts we are deeply indebted. Ferdinand Christian Baur has thrown floods of light on the New Testament literature. Are we to reject that light because his mind was unhappily prejudiced by Hegelianism? Stade gives to the History of Ancient Israel a freshness and a vividness which make our Old Testament fascinating as a new Story. Are we to lose all that stimulus because his mind is vitiated with the strange delusion that the supernatural is *à priori* impossible? No, why may we not accept what he gives us, always making allowance for that mental obliquity which he shares with many unspiritual persons?

If this little book has any claim to public notice it is on the ground that in it an attempt has been made to show the abiding foundations of the Bible, unmoved and immoveable, and at the same time to recognize and allow for all the facts which the acute and earnest study of a generation of Biblical scholars has brought to light.

Perhaps I may add a word to Agnostics or Rationalists, if these pages should come under their notice. The thoughtful unbeliever of the present day sees no middle course between the unthinking credulity of the great mass of believers, who accept the Bible just as Mohammedans accept the Koran, and who seem to think—

> *Credo*, that is the door of Heaven,
>   The more incredible so much more
> Virtue lies in the *Credo* given
>   To open the everlasting door,

he sees, I say, no middle course between this and the rigorous Rationalism which treats the Bible as it treats any other book, and concludes, from the first, that it is not different from the Sacred Literatures of other Religions.

Now the plain fact I wish to urge on the Agnostic's attention is this: that when we do treat the Bible as any other book, with an unprejudiced mind, *then and not till then its astounding intrinsic difference from all other Sacred Literatures begins to appear.* The following pages may open his eyes to this fact which is constantly suggested, though not in a full sense demonstrated, by all that is there said. The more unthinking infidelity which exists so widely among our working people may, I venture to hope, receive a check when it becomes aware that the facts which it thinks it has discovered for the first time in the Bible are well known to Biblical scholars, and that, making full allowance for these, admitting all the light which can be thrown on the History as history, and on the Literature as literature, we rise from our study more convinced than ever that the Bible is God's Book, and that it is *inspired*, not in the mean mechanical sense which is alone recognized in most infidel writings, but in a wide and deep sense, which it is difficult to define just because it is God's way instead of man's way, and therefore, like God's way in Nature, inscrutable and high—"we cannot attain unto it."

I cannot let these pages go forth without expressing my obligation to my friend, Mr. Joseph King, whose careful revision and many suggestions have in all cases lightened my labour, and in some largely shaped the results.

HAMPSTEAD, *Feb.*, 1888.

CONTENTS.

CHAPTER I.
THE MEANING OF INSPIRATION 1

CHAPTER II.
THE EPISTLE IN THE INSPIRED BOOK . . . 25

CHAPTER III.
THE BIOGRAPHIES OF THE INSPIRED BOOK . . 56

CHAPTER IV.
THE NEW TESTAMENT IN GENERAL . . . 96

CHAPTER V.
THE OLD TESTAMENT: THE PROPHET IN THE INSPIRED BOOK 113

CHAPTER VI.
THE HISTORY IN THE INSPIRED BOOK . . . 138

CHAPTER VII.

THE LAW 176

CHAPTER VIII.

THE POETRY AND THE MISCELLANEOUS WRITINGS
OF THE INSPIRED BOOK 205

CHAPTER IX.

SUMMARY AND CONCLUSION 234

INDEX 251

INSPIRATION AND THE BIBLE.

CHAPTER I.

ON THE MEANING OF INSPIRATION.

ALL of us—that is to say all who call themselves or wish to be called Christians—agree in saying that the Bible is inspired. But when we begin to ask,' On what ground do we rest our assertion? or, What precisely do we mean by being inspired? immediately we seem to hear in place of the unanimous agreement a babel of confused and conflicting opinions. Then we fall into parties, and abuse one another, and each party says that the opposite party is undermining the belief in inspiration, by which it means that the opposite party rests on a different ground and holds a different view concerning the meaning of the word. All the time, however, the contending parties are quite agreed in the main belief that the Scriptures are inspired, and might easily understand one another and unite the elements of truth which each has got hold of, if only they would clear their ideas and state them with precision. For truth, as Bacon says, emerges more readily from error than from confusion.

On what ground do we believe that the Bible is inspired? Some will give the ready answer, 'We believe that the Bible is inspired *because the Church says so.*' As a High Church writer on the Canon puts it, "he should give no more credit to Matthew than to Livy unless the Church obliged him." This is a very intelligible answer for those who are not troubled with a previous question, ' On what ground must I accept the authority of the Church ?' But the answer is a little hard and mechanical. It is very much as if we were to say, as in effect a good many people actually do say, ' We believe in Milton's poetical genius, because the great universal literary judgment of two centuries or more has maintained it.' The drawback of such a view will be that we shall very likely allow Milton's poetical genius to rest upon that foundation without any very fresh or serious examination of the question for ourselves. In the same way, when we say that we accept the Inspiration of the Bible because the Church declares it, we are very much disposed to listen to what the Church says on other things rather than to what the Inspired Book says ; for we instinctively feel that the Authority which establishes our authority must have more weight than the authority that is established. And, to take the extreme case, for some centuries the

Church Authority which anthorized the inspired Scriptures actually withdrew them from the people, until at last they seemed to break their way through, and to utter their voice for themselves in a way which did not tend to confirm the Church Authority. We are not, however, attempting to criticise; we are only attempting to state some of the grounds on which different groups of people declare that the Bible is inspired.

Some will give as their ground a well-used, and we may add an ill-used, text from the Second Epistle to Timothy (iii. 15, 16) which reads in the Authorized Version, "from a child thou hast known the Holy Scriptures, which are able to make thee wise unto salvation through faith which is in Christ Jesus. All scripture is given by inspiration of God, and is profitable for doctrine, for reproof, for correction, for instruction in righteousness." We need not perplex ourselves with the uncertainty of the rendering, which is at once apparent when we turn to the original Greek, or to the Revised Version. But it is plain that this verse could only apply to what was held as Holy Scripture when the verse was written; it could not apply, for instance, to the Second Epistle to Timothy itself, which was at that time being written, still less to those books of the New Testament which were not yet written, or which, being written, had not yet been gathered into a 'Canon' so as to come under the head of 'Holy Scriptures.' In fact the more this famous verse is considered in all its bearings, the more it will appear that, while it may serve to express very well our idea of what is meant by the Inspired Bible, it cannot possibly be the *ground* on which we believe that the Bible, Old and New Testaments combined, as we possess it, is inspired. But here again we must not stop to criticise this very general view. We simply state it.

Others there are who, when asked why they believe the Bible to be inspired, would reply, 'It is because we have found it to be so practically; by reading it we found our way to God; by searching it the will of God has become clearer to us; by living according to its precepts we have proved that they are Divine; and now its words move us as no other words do: other books delight us, instruct us, thrill us, but this Book is a Prophetic Voice discoursing about Eternity and the Unseen in the same breath that it speaks with a demonstrable truthfulness concerning the Temporal and the Seen.' And further, they may add, 'we have found the key to the Book in the Person to whom the Book points all along, Jesus Christ; in the Book He is presented to us; we see the ages travailing with the hope of Him, history leading up to Him, prophet and poet dimly or clearly speaking of Him; at last He Himself appears moving on the plane of History, and taking possession of the Kingdoms of the World.' The people who answer in this way certainly seem to render a more solid reason than those who found their assertion about inspiration upon the Tradition of an authoritative Church, or than those who try to show that the Bible is inspired because a text in the Bible itself says that Holy Scripture is given by inspiration.

But we need not lay any stress upon the greater conclusiveness of this third answer to the question. The point which strikes us is that Christians are more certain that the Bible is inspired than they are of the grounds of their certainty. And generally speaking it is a mistake to dismiss an assertion as untrue merely because the grounds on which it is made are insufficient. An old Indian official advised a young Indian judge always "to give his verdict, but to avoid giving the grounds of it." And this remark applies still more forcibly to a widely held popular belief, such as the belief in God, or the belief in immortality, or the belief in the Inspiration of the Bible. The belief may be well grounded, and yet no one who holds it may be adequately able to state the grounds, and all the statements put together and harmonized may still leave one in some astonishment how a conviction so sure and so momentous should rest upon so slender and wavering a foundation.

We must not, then, be held to be unreasonable if in the inquiry which we are to institute in the following pages we start with the traditional belief in the Inspiration of the Bible. We take what the Latin language calls the *common sense* of Christians in all ages and in all places, which asserts that the

Bible is inspired, and we are not greatly disturbed if one states as his ground that the Church says so, and another that his fathers said so, and another that the Bible itself teaches it, and another that his own inward conviction is his authority, and another that the Spirit of God revealed it to him. We disregard the reasons for the present, but accept the belief which *seems* to rest upon these diverse reasons. We have in our hands an Inspired Book, and we want to know what we are to do with it, and first of all we want to know what we mean by the word Inspired.

What is Inspiration? We can hardly say that we have not asked ourselves the question, but many of us can say that we have been content to ask it and have never seriously attempted to give an answer to it. Thus it frequently happens that a vague idea of Inspiration crystallizes round some definite thought, and gradually we find we have got a hard and fast statement of what Inspiration is, to which we imagine the Bible must conform, because, as we are all agreed, it is inspired. But if this crystallized idea happens to be wrong, if the Bible therefore does not conform to it, then we are clearly in great danger. If we are very confident in our faith, then we are apt to try to shut our eyes to the facts of the Bible which do not conform to our idea, to distort them, to allegorize them, or in the last resort to explain them away. If on the other hand we are wavering in our faith, finding that the facts in the Bible do not conform to our idea of Inspiration, oddly enough we are disposed to say that the Bible is not inspired rather than to doubt whether our theory of inspiration could be right. In the first case we become Biblical Bigots; in the second case we become Sceptics, and unless some wise friend is at hand to show us our mistake, absolute Unbelievers.

An illustration taken from a former page of religious history will set the danger here referred to in a clear light. The Rabbinical students of the Old Testament, engaged in an exclusive and minute study of their sacred writings, gradually formed an idea of Inspiration which it appears to us almost incredible that any reasonable person could entertain. From the time of Ezra we can very clearly trace the growth of this theory. At first it was believed that the *Law* came from God —by the Law was understood the definite commandments contained in the Law; then it was maintained that the whole book containing the Law came from God; then it was maintained that the Pentateuch was written from beginning to end at the dictation of God, Moses writing in a kind of dream. "He who says that Moses," ran the dogma, "wrote even one verse of his own knowledge, is a denier and despiser of the Word of God." The closing verses of Deuteronomy which recount the death of Moses and add, 'there arose not a prophet since in Israel like unto Moses' (Deut. xxxiv. 10), occasioned no difficulty; Moses had by a prophetic insight written this account of his own funeral and this epitaph to record his permanent position in Israel. But even this was not enough; the final rabbinical view declared that God did not dictate while Moses wrote, but He handed the Law in a visible and tangible form out of Heaven; and the only question disputed was whether He gave it in one volume at one time, or in several volumes at several times.

It is curious to notice how this rabbinical view of inspiration influenced the Early Church thinkers on the subject, and actually appeared in the Reformation of the Sixteenth Century, when distracted Protestantism was seeking for some simple and final authority to set over against the discredited authority of the infallible Pope. Dr. John Owen, for instance, in common with many others, equally good, if not equally learned, in his own day, boldly maintained that the vowel-points in the Hebrew Scriptures were inspired, though it is beyond all question that they were never written until Hebrew had ceased to be generally spoken by the Jews, and it became necessary to fix the traditional vocalization. Now just to dwell for a moment on the danger involved in such a dogma. The meaning of obscure passages is at once restored to us in many cases when the right vowel-pointing is restored by conjecture; but let us suppose that a man has included in his idea of Inspiration the absolute and infallible correctness of the traditional vowel-points, he will be in this curious position that his faith in the Scripture is shaken directly the sense is made out; the meaningless passage was inspired; the discovery of its meaning is an assault on Inspiration.

In the case of the Rabbinical dogma, which seems to us very absurd, we see at once what a peril is prepared for us so soon as the text is carefully studied. A slight error in figures, a misspelling of a name, becomes a charge against the penmanship of God. But we do not so readily see how a false conception of Inspiration, though not so flagrant as this, may in its degree be preparing serious dangers for us when the extension of knowledge throws a new light upon the Sacred Writings. If we have included in our idea of Inspiration a faultless accuracy in the use of terms describing natural phenomena, we may be driven, as many have been driven, to maintain that the earth is the centre of the universe and the sun revolves round it, because the Bible makes use of the popular language on the subject. If we have included in our idea of Inspiration an intention to supersede the researches of physical science, we may be driven, as many have been driven, to close our eyes to the surest conclusions of geology or biology; in doing which we certainly pay a high compliment to our idea of Inspiration, but it is doubtful whether we render much service to the Inspired Book. Or if, once more, we have included in our idea of Inspiration a guarantee against any historical inaccuracy, then indeed we are in a dire perplexity if historical monuments show us that some errors exist in the

Sacred Writings, or still more if we find the Sacred Writings themselves containing two or more versions of the same event which are, strictly speaking, unreconcilable. Under such circumstances, we try to shut our eyes, or we open them and our faith is shaken. It is, then, a very important matter not only to put to ourselves the question, What is Inspiration? but to get a clear answer to it; so that we may not in a vague way form a conception which is likely to land us in difficulties and dangers such as these which have just been referred to. Now the answer to our question is not so hard to get as might appear at first sight, if we will only be quite candid, and if we are willing to bestow some patience in going whither our candour leads us. In fact the answer to our question lies quite ready to hand. *We mean by Inspiration exactly those qualities and characteristics which are the marks or notes of the Bible.* We do not mean what the Greeks meant by the inspiration of the Delphic prophetess, the wild, excited, obscure, ambiguous utterance of a woman in religious phrenzy. We do not mean what the Rabbis meant by the Inspiration of Moses who "did not write one verse of his own knowledge." We do not mean what the Mohammedans mean when they speak of the inspiration of the Koran, for there is all the difference in the world between a book written by one man, and a book composed of writings which cover nearly 1500 years. We mean by Inspiration precisely that which is the note of our Sacred Scriptures. It is a word *sui generis*. It is a term which has only one thing for its content. It is true we use the word in other connections also; for instance, we speak of the *inspiration* of a great action when a man rises above himself; but no one for a moment confuses that use of the word with Inspiration as applied to Scripture. More confusing perhaps is the language we sometimes use about great writers, poets, and preachers, when we say that they are inspired. But a moment's reflection shows us that the word means something quite different when it is employed to express the effect which men of genius produce upon us. We call them inspired because they see more than we do, but not more than we can. They reveal the unobserved to us, but not the unknown or the unknowable. But we call the Bible inspired because it reveals another Order, a Kingdom of Heaven, a view of human nature and of human destiny which lies quite beyond our ken. There is poetry in the Bible of a high order; but it is not as poets that we call the writers of Isaiah lv. and 1 Cor. xiii. inspired; it is as revealers of God, of God's purposes, of God's methods. It is not so much the unobserved, it is the unknown, the otherwise unknowable, that they reveal to us.

And so with great preachers and teachers, Emerson, Carlyle, Ruskin, Browning, Frederick Robertson, Thomas Lynch, we quickly recognize that their inspiration comes from having drunk deeply of the spirit of the Inspired Book; and where they speak of themselves and are only inspired in the secondary sense, we miss what we may call the note of the Bible, the note of Revelation in the highest sense. Thus if we are strict with ourselves and insist on a rigorous use of words, we shall find more and more that Inspiration as applied to the Bible is a term applicable only to the Bible. It is the word, not perhaps the best word, but a word consecrated by long usage, which serves to express that peculiar impression which the Sacred Scriptures carry with them. It is not so much this or that verse or saying which is *inspired;* it is the "All Scripture," it is this sacred Canon of books, which has remained in the Church from the beginning, ' profitable for teaching, for reproof, for correction, for instruction which is in righteousness.'

To the question, then, What is Inspiration? we have to answer, Precisely that which the Bible *is*.

But when once this simple truth is realized, and cleared from all the illusion of false ideas which have been the growth of centuries, we find the task which lies before us is, though arduous and long, yet full of hope and promise. Relieved from the incubus of a big falsity, we can turn joyfully to the discovery of the truth. To find out what is the content of the term Inspiration, we must set to work earnestly and diligently to find out what the Bible actually is. Instead of being hampered in all our inquiries by a foregone conclusion, and frightened from a candid investigation of fact by the fear lest the fact should shatter our theory of Inspiration, we go to form our theory of Inspiration from an examination of the facts. To use the language of Logic, our inquiry becomes Inductive instead of Deductive; it is Positive instead of Metaphysical. The time, then, to formulate a doctrine of Inspiration is when we have fairly and freely and fully investigated all that the Inspired Volume contains; only then can we draw together the varied phenomena and attempt to give an idea of the term not merely by example but by definition. We may, however, for clearness' and convenience' sake, adopt a formula at the outset which we hold subject to revision. We may express it thus. *We call our Bible inspired, by which we mean that by reading it and studying it we find our way to God, we find His will for us, and we find how we can conform ourselves to His will.*

This is our starting-point. But before we begin to map out the course by which we must go, perhaps we ought to meet an objection which many are likely to urge. We may be told that this Inductive Method of arriving at Inspiration leaves us without a theory at all until we have finished the investigation, and further that it leaves every reader to reach his own conclusion about the Inspired Volume and lands us in all the diversities and miseries of private judgment. Certainly this seems a serious objection. Indeed we have lived so long with a cast-iron theory of Inspiration round our neck, that we may very possibly feel quite uncomfortable to be without it; and the diversities and miseries of private judgment may well horrify us all, especially if we have no understanding of that saying, 'Where the Spirit of the Lord is there is liberty.' But nevertheless the objection is not so serious as it seems, and it loses much of its force when the objections on the other side are taken into account. For it must be owned that the method of having a cast-iron theory of inspiration to start with has not been wholly successful. We have multitudes among us who have thrown their Bibles away, or are using them only as the *corpus vile* to flog and to deride. We have only to glance at the literature which issues from the infidel press to see that to our working men at least, the part of the community for whom Christ's religion is peculiarly adapted, the cast-iron theory has rendered no very signal service. From it and it alone in almost every case comes the first difficulty to the young mechanic who is just beginning to think for himself. To it is due first the sceptical suspicion and last the utter rejection of the Book; and when the poor secularist after years of vainly beating the air is brought back again to truth and reality, it is by the living Christ, whom he might have known and loved from the first but for the wrong lines on which he was set by the cast-iron theory. He lost His Saviour because he found Jeremiah saying, 'O Lord, thou hast deceived me' (xx. 7), and concluded that the Bible taught a God who is a deceiver; or because he found King Lemuel saying

(Prov. xxxi. 6), 'Give strong drink unto him that is ready to perish, and wine unto the bitter in soul; let him drink and forget his poverty and remember his misery no more,' and he thought that the Bible countenanced the drinking practices which are the curse of his country. No, the cast-iron method has not been a success, as the infidel propaganda very clearly proves. And whether the educated classes have benefited by it is very questionable. It has made some read the Bible and so brought them to Faith; but it has made many others read the Bible and so brought them to Doubt. It may not then, on the whole, be at all a bad thing for some of us if we have to hold our theory of Inspiration in suspense until we have studied the Inspired writings: for while it may rob parts of the Bible teaching of a certain adventitious authority, on the other hand it will not give an adventitious authority to other passages which are constantly misunderstood and consequently misleading. This part of the objection may be held balanced by the objection on the other side.

Then as to the miseries of private judgment, we are in Modern Europe so committed to them that we are well-nigh bound to face them; and after all, when the alternatives are considered we perhaps shall not hesitate which to choose. On the one hand we are required to accept on authority a given theory of Inspiration, for which we see no adequate grounds, and which seeming to us intrinsically unreasonable loses all interest, so that if we accept it at all we accept it only in a quiescent and listless way. On the other hand we are to have a theory of Inspiration which may not be identically the same with that of others; each of us will be in a slightly different position on the subject; but what we have attained we shall hold fast; it will be for us living and real. In this as in most other cases a very little faith of *our own* is worth ten times the quantity of other people's It is not by having a large and complex belief, but by fully and intelligently holding what belief is ours that spiritual knowledge and spiritual life increase. So that on the whole the objection to the Inductive Method of finding out what Inspiration is need not alarm us. We may take the method and turn to examine the course by which we are to go, determined at least that our belief shall be a real belief, and that if we give an answer at all to the questions which arise it shall be our own answer and not another's.

The task which lies before us is to examine what the Inspired Book actually is, to take into account all the circumstances of its origin and making which come under our notice, to observe all its distinguishing features, its characteristics, in a word to examine it with the tenderness and enthusiasm which a scientific investigator always feels for his subject matter. The parallel of the physical scientist may help us if we consider it for a moment. The physiologist does not feel that he is irreverent in dissecting the organism on the table before him and in tracing out with the minutest care the connection of parts, the ramification of nerves, and even the primitive formation and development of cells; the botanist, again, takes his flower to pieces out of love for it, every feature of stem, ovary and corolla, is examined under the microscope. It is the man who has no love for these things that leaves them untouched and we attach very little weight to the protestation of the careless medical student that he has too much reverence for an organism to dissect it, or to the sentimental indifference of a fox-hunter that he is too fond of the flowers of the field to pull them to pieces under the microscope. It is not therefore irreverence towards the Sacred Book which prompts us, if we may so speak, to dissect it, to examine its details, and to spare no labour in understanding all that we can about it. It is rather the profound conviction of its eternal and immutable truth which leads men to deal with it in this way; it is a poor tribute of reverence to abstain from all close inquiry, as if we feared that under such an inquiry its pretentions would crumble away.

What makes this searching investigation the more necessary and the more interesting is that our Book is almost in all respects the exact opposite of what we should antecedently have required an Inspired Volume to be. We should have asked for a neat and clear statement of a creed or of a doctrine, drawn up under heads, and enforced with direct and forcible applications; we should have expected that this handy Text Book of revelation should be handed to us from Heaven somewhat in the manner in which the Rabbis would have it that the Law was given to Moses. What we actually have is a volume composed of two compressed literatures, the literature of an ancient people, history, poetry, and preaching, and the literature of an early religious movement, biography, letters, and visions. Instead of the clear formulation of a creed there is the long growth and transmutation of a religion. Instead of deliberate treatises on doctrine, there are occasional pieces of all sorts, utterances of prophets which were addressed only to the people among whom they lived, and have long ceased to have anything but a historical or an exemplary interest, bursts of lyric song evoked by national sorrows which have long lain in the tomb of history, letters written to meet pressing emergencies and to answer unexpected problems which presented themselves in the circle of a young community.

That these two literatures bound together in our Bible have a unity and a connection with one another is plain enough from this, that for generations men have read the Bible as if it were an Inspired Book of a thoroughly human type, all written by one pen, at one sitting, at the dictation of God. That is the marvel of it. But now there has come to us the deeply interesting work of breaking up this Unity, examining the constituent parts, the developments, the evolutions, and so discovering what an Inspired Book of a thoroughly Divine type is, and how wholly it differs from one of a thoroughly human type. We are called on to unfold this volume of Hebrew literature ; to distinguish the several historical sources which 'unite in its narratives, to examine so far as may be the authorship of each work in the collection, to determine when the author lived, who he was, by what circumstances he was surrounded ; and when all these questions are answered to the best of our ability, we turn to observe with a fresh wonder and delight how each writing seems to fill its foreordained niche in the library, to stand as a prepared stone in a large mosaic. We are called on to peruse the smaller volume of Christian literature, to affix the author's name to each writing, the date and the occasion, or if this be impossible, to comprehend the bearings of a writing whose authorship, date, and occasion remain unknown ; and here again as our task reaches a conclusion we marvel how these diverse writings, presenting so many different phases of Christian thought and feeling, combine to create a tolerably distinct and unified impression of the Faith and the Practice which the Son of Man instituted in the world.

It does not fall within the scope of the present little volume to systematically examine each book of the Bible in the way that has just been suggested. Not only would that take us too far, but the opinions of scholars are still wavering upon many most interesting questions connected with the date and authorship of several parts of the Bible. All that we can do is to touch the question at certain salient points, and suggest the ways in which the investigation might be carried out to completeness. But it may be possible to lay stress on one thing; if the view here taken of Inspiration and the way of regarding it be accepted, we can afford to bear ourselves with very great composure towards those workers in the field of the Higher Criticism whose labours have affrighted many weak minds and sent a shock of indignation to hearts that are not given to excited feeling. The Higher Criticism, or the scientific investigation of the authorship, composition, dates and occasions of the Bible writings, can only be our friend. It cannot rob us of our inspired Scriptures; there they will be, when it has done its best, shining upon us like the quiet stars when the surf and the drift of the storm have passed away. All it can do, all it wishes to do, is to tell us the truth about our Scriptures. Its hypothetical theories, its extravagant conjectures, the excesses into which young speculative Sciences always run, will be quietly moderated by the sure prevalence of truth. Its clearly established results less or more will be an unmixed gain to us all; they will not destroy our idea of Inspiration; we shall in future include them in our idea of Inspiration. The alarm which has been created in England and Scotland by the mooting of questions which have been familiar to German Theology for a generation, does not speak very well for the robustness of our faith or for the lucidity of our ideas. Even now most of us are a little ashamed of our panic, and are turning to the great scholars who have led the way in this field to enlighten us, instead of anathematizing them and bidding them begone. And already many of us are rubbing our eyes and wondering how we could ever have supposed that a thing so true, so solid, so present, so enduring, so large with promise, so sure of the future as the Kingdom of Heaven which Christ came to establish, would be overthrown from its foundations if it were shown that the Pentateuch as we have it could not have come from the pen of Moses, or even that some of the letters which have passed as Paul's in all probability have another authorship. For this alarm, of which we are beginning to be ashamed, the cast-iron theory of Inspiration is no doubt largely to blame; we did not think that the Hebrew vowel-points were inspired perhaps, but we thought that the headings of our chapters and the titles of the books certainly must be.

It remains in this chapter only to point out what we must try to do in the succeeding chapters; where our investigation is to begin and where it is to end. We have already seen that we have two Literatures bound up in one volume. It would seem natural to begin with the earlier and so pass on to the later; but that course is by no means to be commended; by following that course many of the most serious misuses of the Scriptures have arisen ; by following that course we have seen nations and churches making the Jewish law and the Jewish faith their standard of conduct and teaching, quite forgetting that it is the Jewish Law and Faith and Polity transmuted in the doctrine and the work of Christ with which we nowadays have to do. Our course then is to begin with the Christian Literature as our starting point, and to work back to its origin and its preparations in the Old Testament religion. The apostles themselves, it is true, and the early apologists like Justin Martyr, used the Old Testament as their text-book in preaching Christianity ; but then several things must be taken into account. In the first place the apostles were Jews speaking to Jews, and the ancient Scriptures were their common ground. But in the second place the use they made of the ancient Scriptures was determined by the fulfilment they saw of the Law in Him who was the end of the Law ; it was the Old Testament interpreted by the Apostolic Spirit which was the text-book of the early Christian preachers ; but that apostolic spirit, and that apostolic witness is precisely what is permanently retained for us in the New Testament. To use our Bibles rightly, therefore, we may lay it down as a fixed canon that we must always look back upon the Old Testament from the standpoint of the New; we are not to depreciate the root from which the tree sprang, but we are always to remember that it is the tree and not the root with which we are in the first instance concerned. It was the dangerous reversal of this proper Christian method which led some Christian teachers, like Marcion, travelling on the lines of reaction, to entirely repudiate the Jewish Scriptures, and to found their teaching solely on the Christian Literature. This was a great mistake, it is true, but it is better to have the New Testament alone, than to have a whole Bible with the Old Testament overshadowing the New, as the larger and the foremost shadows and obscures the smaller which comes after. We may settle it then that our first business is to investigate the New Testament, to grasp and take into account all the phenomena which present themselves there, that our theory of Inspiration may not exclude any of them; to find out all we can about the authorship, date, and occasions, of the several writings, and, where that is impossible, to adjust the bearings of the writings of unknown origin. All that can be done in the present volume is to take two features, first an Epistle, and then the Histories, and in examining them to point out the lines on which examination of the rest would proceed.

Then we must turn back to the Old Testament, and touching there the four groups, Prophecy, History, the Law, and the Poetry, we may get a clue to the understanding of all by taking examples in each.

Then having suggested the directions in which the investigations seem to lead us, we may be able to draw together a certain number of ascertained facts which are to be taken into account and allowed to shape our conception of Inspiration.

It is a pleasant field which lies before us, and we are not harassed by the fear that if we search it we may lose it. We may see reason as we proceed to dismiss some ideas which we have accepted from tradition, and to change others; but whatever may present itself to our eyes, one thing will stand not only sure, but made doubly sure, " The Law of the Lord is perfect, restoring the soul: the testimony of the Lord is sure, making wise the simple." Nay, we may with some confidence predict that as the great vista of the Bible opens out to us, and the atmosphere of reality begins to show us the right perspective of its parts, we shall find a new and strange meaning in our Lord's saying that "one jot or one tittle shall in no wise pass from the law till all be fulfilled." It is the man who is bound by a rigid Authority, or the man who is held in a blinding traditionalism, and not the free and fair investigator, that has to leave out of account innumerable jots and tittles of the Law which can find no place in his theory. There are parts of the Bible we may conjecture which are never read by certain good Christian people, lest their theory of Inspiration might be shaken; there are parts which the same people would wish removed but that they count the wish blasphemous. We need fear no such chilling doubts in ranging through this pleasant field that is before us.

CHAPTER II.

ON THE EPISTLE IN THE INSPIRED BOOK.

LET us look round and see in what position we are left by the preceding chapter. We have an Inspired Book before us, but we are not yet clear as to what must be included in our idea of Inspiration. We must therefore examine the structure, the making, the details of the Book, and as every fact emerges into sight we must take account of it, settling it with ourselves that our idea of Inspiration must be wide enough to embrace this new fact. Further, we have seen reason for beginning our inquiry with the later, or Christian literature, rather than with the earlier, or Jewish literature. We concentrate our attention for the time upon the New Testament, and we turn to examine its composition, its dates, its occasions.

We are disposed at first to begin with the Gospels. For purposes of instruction in the faith, the biographies of Jesus and the story of Peter's and Paul's acts are rightly placed foremost in the New Testament; but for our purposes this will not be the most fruitful starting-point. Our starting-point must be the Letters which are grouped together as coming from the pen of St. Paul, fourteen in number. The reason for beginning with these is that they are the earliest compositions of the Christian literature which have come down to us. The materials of the Gospels are, it is true, earlier by twenty or thirty years; but here we are concerned with the literary side of the question; the earliest writings, not the earliest events, are what we want to consider. Another advantage in starting from this point is that we are starting from writings about the authorship of which there is little or no question. But when we say that there is no question about Paul being the writer of these letters, we must draw a distinction. It is very questionable whether the Epistle to the Hebrews was written by Paul; or rather we may say it is very certain that it was not. It does not claim to be his; the style is certainly not his, and there seems no reason whatever for maintaining that it is his. Then the three letters to Timothy and Titus cause great difficulty, not only because of their contents, but also because in the life of the apostle, as it is known to us, there is actually no point at which we can place them; consequently they require us to imagine some further years added to his life, of which we have none but traditional notices. Again, there are the letters to the Ephesians and the Colossians; in the present state of criticism we are hardly justified in assuming that they were written by St. Paul without entering into a long discussion; though we may notice in passing that they afford an apt illustration of the way in which the spiritual value of a composition may remain unaffected by the question of authorship; they who have drunk most deeply of the spirit of those wonderful letters would never dream of saying that their value depended on the question whether St. Paul wrote them or not. Their value is an intrinsic value. Their vision into the things unseen, and their presentation of the work and the person of Christ, remain a possession for the Church, a light and an instruction, a revelation, though the writer should be some unknown disciple of the great apostle who wrote as he was moved by the Holy Ghost, but preferred to write under the name of his master rather than obtruding his own personality. There then come four other letters in the collection, First and Second Thessalonians, Philippians and Philemon, which only a hypercriticism ventures to dissociate from the pen of the apostle. Yet, because hypercriticism still raises questions and does not confess that the questions are fully met, it will be more convenient for our purpose to take refuge in the four undisputed letters. That the Epistles to the Galatians, the Corinthians, and the Romans were actually written by Paul, and have come down to us essentially unaltered, is practically beyond question.

Here then we have a safe and sound starting-point. Master these four letters, and you have a base of operations for turning to settle the more disputable points in the New Testament literature.

Before we decide which of the four letters shall serve as our example of the method of treatment, we may pause to observe and to emphasize that no judgment has been finally passed upon the authorship of the other ten Epistles. We leave the question *sub judice ;* and we must remind ourselves how entirely free we are to do so on the principle laid down in the first chapter. But there are some to whom this remark will seem startling and dangerous: so accustomed have they been to accept the headings of the books of the Bible as *inspired*, by which they mean infallibly accurate, that it seems to them as if in losing the authorship of Paul they would be losing the writings themselves. Very possibly they have read these letters and drawn daily strength from them without ever thinking for a moment about Paul, or in any way connecting the effect they have produced with his personal character, or with his particular authorship ; yet they have an uneasy feeling that should the name of Paul be withdrawn from the letters, all their value and authority would instantly vanish away. We may say confidently that there is no fear of this ; just as there was no fear of the moon ceasing to shine when it was discovered that her light was not her own, but reflected. The 'Inspiration' of these letters is the Spirit of God, not the Apostle Paul, speaking through them. 'But,' exclaims the anxious and puzzled Bible reader, 'this questioning of Pauline authorship would represent the letters as forgeries and impostures!' The answer to that difficulty is to be found in the better knowledge of the literary practice of the Ancient World. It is perfectly certain that a disciple of St. Paul's, anxious to communicate his master's teaching to the Churches, would not hesitate to veil his own hand under the form of a letter from his master; what we should call 'forgery' he would call modesty. We know that Paul wrote generally by means of an amanuensis. Sometimes, it may be, the letters were not so much dictated as given in epitome, for the faithful friend and follower to write in full. When the master was himself gone there would remain many of these notes, flashes of inspired thought, messages to particular Churches, directions to individuals, which a reverent disciple might set down and publish as a Pauline letter. There is nothing improbable in the supposition that, when the letters were collected from the several Churches to form the Canon of the apostle's writings, some of these secondary letters, as we may call them, should have been included as in the style and spirit of the master. Sometimes even, by a bolder step still, a writer might purposely cast the convictions and practice of the Churches of his own day in the form of a letter addressed by the great apostle to one of his beloved communities, or to one of his faithful disciples.

We need not, however, pursue the question at

length. No harm will be done in our maintaining that all the fourteen letters were written by St. Paul, so long as we clearly see, and stoutly maintain, that should the fact prove to be otherwise, we could and would accept it, knowing that the truth could not rob us of our real possessions. In turning our attention to the four undisputed letters, we are able to take the personality and the circumstances of the writer into our account; and on a closer investigation it will appear that these four letters are, roughly speaking, distinguished by this, that the personality and circumstances of the writer form a considerable element of their value. There are some books, narrative poems, histories, philosophical treatises, which have an impersonal significance; whoever wrote them it is much the same to the reader. There are other books, autobiographies, correspondence, personal experiences, which would lose all meaning if we ignored the writer. There is just this distinction between the letter to the Ephesians, for example, and the letter to the Galatians.

Having narrowed our inquiry for the present to the four undisputed letters of St. Paul, the question arises, Which of the four shall we select for examination, to serve as an example of method for the rest, since we cannot attempt to deal thoroughly with all? Let us select the Epistle to the Galatians: it has several striking advantages from our point of view. For one thing, it is in all probability the earliest of the four; for another thing, it is the briefest and the simplest; and lastly, it contains a passage of autobiography which may be taken as a middle-point and standard for the discussion of the historical questions which arise in the study of the New Testament. It is true, as will already be clear from our rapid survey of the fourteen Epistles, that each one of them requires a separate examination, and what applies to one may not apply to all; but at the same time if we can succeed in thinking ourselves into the circumstances which gave rise to this one letter; if we can succeed in looking over the apostle's shoulder as he wrote it; if we can discern the mingling of Divine and human elements in the composition; if we can mark the limitations which are necessarily imposed by the circumstances and the personality of the author; and if, finally, we can grasp the universal significance which this apparently occasional piece has for the Church and for the world, we shall have got a very good idea of how we should set about the investigation of the other letters, and how we should bring together the gross results of a complete examination of them all.

We may with some confidence fix the date of our Epistle. Without entering into minute controversies which in this connection hardly concern us, we may say that Paul wrote from Ephesus some time during those two years which are mentioned in the tenth verse of the nineteenth chapter of the Acts, the two years of ministry in the school of Tyrannus. These two years must be sought between A.D. 54 and A.D. 58 ; and we may without surrendering our judgment to authority be content to accept the year 57 as the year in which this letter which lies in our hands to-day was actually written. This outward point agreed upon, we have now to turn inwards and examine the letter itself: and certainly it leaves little to be desired in its vividness and reality. Taking it in our hands, we turn to the brief itinerary records of the Acts, "they went through the region of Phrygia and Galatia, having been forbidden of the Holy Ghost to speak the word in Asia" (Acts xvi. 6, A.D. 52), and "having spent some time there (at Antioch), he departed and went through the region of Galatia and Phrygia in order, stablishing all the disciples" (Acts xviii. 23 ; this was just before his arrival and settlement at Ephesus), and the dry notices are suddenly filled with life and meaning, and we cannot help wishing that we had such a commentary as this upon every statement in the book of the Acts of the Apostles. It is the difference between the record in the parish books of birth and death, and the autobiography which makes the name a man and the empty years a life. What colour comes into that first visit to Galatia, when we find the apostle describing it thus, "Ye know that because of an infirmity of the flesh"—possibly a violent attack of ophthalmia, the disease which like a thorn in the flesh embittered his life, disfigured his person, and made his handwriting a scrawl—"I preached the gospel unto you the first time, and that which was a temptation to you in my flesh ye despised not, nor spat out, but ye received me as an angel of God even as Christ Jesus"; and again, "for I bear you witness that if possible ye would have plucked out your eyes and given them to me" (Gal. iv. 13–15). Here at once we are in the tide of actual events; we are with the weary and suffering missionary forced to stop in his journey because of illness, finding himself among a new race, volatile, emotional Celts, rousing himself to preach the Word, to drop a seed by the wayside, standing before the people, the visibly excitable people, himself an object of derision, if not of loathing. We feel the throb of his heart as in his infirmity of the flesh he "openly sets forth Jesus Christ crucified" before his audience; he forgets himself; he is himself crucified with Christ; the people are touched; they too forget the external disfigurements, and see only in the transformed person of the apostle an angel of God, a manifestation of Christ Himself. With passionate enthusiasm they crowd around him. Any one of them is ready to change eyes with him, if only it were possible; to take from him the diseased tormented eyes which at first had struck them with disgust; in fact to make any sacrifice for one who had brought them so wonderful and saving a message.

But the occasion of the letter is not to praise

the enthusiastic people; it is to warn and to reproach them. The second visit recorded in the Acts had been disappointing; the glow had died away; there was a certain chill in their manner; they treated him as if he had "become their enemy" (iv. 16). When he dealt plainly with them, they resented it. While he "stablished the disciples" he noticed counter-currents which he had not time to stop and overcome. Arrived in Ephesus, he had further intelligence of his "churches of Galatia"; it was not reassuring. Other influences had been at work amongst them. Men of Jewish birth had come preaching another gospel, declaring that Christian faith without Jewish rites was of no avail. They had required the Galatian converts to be circumcised, to conform to the ordinances of the law; in a word to become Jews. They had attempted to discredit the minister of the gospel who had preached Christ to them, declaring that he was not in the apostolic succession, but an unauthorized preacher. It was precisely a similar case to what happens now and again in the modern mission field; people have been won to Christ, have cast away their idols, and are rejoicing in the freedom of the gospel, when missionaries of a Catholic type arrive and assure them that simple faith will profit them nothing unless they submit to certain ordinances which take the place of circumcision, and "observe days and months and seasons and years" (Gal. iv. 10). Paul began to fear that he would have bestowed labour on these Galatian Churches in vain; he saw the Jewish religion threatening the life of "his gospel"; he saw those "who were apostles before him" set up as authorities against him; he saw the freedom wherewith Christ did set them free in danger of destruction from the hands of those who professed to be the immediate disciples and representatives of Christ; he saw the Old Covenant, with its venerable Law, and its venerable Scripture, and its venerable observances, overshadowing the faint fresh growth of the simplicity that is in Christ. An organized Judaism seemed likely to take the place of the Kingdom of God.

The apostle sat down and wrote this eager, passionate expostulation, which is so impetuous in its arguments, so sudden in its appeals and exhortations, so dexterous in its *argumenta ad hominem*, so scathing in its irony, so tender in its love, that it is difficult fully to grasp, but which when once it is grasped leaves an indelible impression, gives us a starting-point for comprehending that early miracle of Christianity, the rapid growth of the gospel and submergence of Judaism. There speaks in every line of this remarkable Epistle, the "servant of Christ" who had been a Jew, and knew all the possibilities of the ancient faith. His first object is to show by turning to his own early history how direct and real the revelation of Jesus Christ had been to him; how independent he felt himself of "those who were reputed to be somewhat," the Apostolic board at Jerusalem. He wants to show that whatever claim might be made for James and Peter and John, the pillars of the Church, it could not be said that Christ was in any way limited to make His revelation through them. Christ could call a man to His apostleship; the Spirit of God could inspire such a man; he might become every whit equal to the pillars of the Church, and yet stand entirely outside of their circle, and entirely repudiate their ordination (ch. i. 12). If Peter was in any way a Primate of the Church, then it was Paul's claim that he had withstood the Primate to the face "because he stood condemned" (Gal. ii. 11). If James was in any way the head of the ancient community at Jerusalem, then it was Paul's privilege to frustrate "certain who came from him" (ii. 12) and to vindicate "the truth of the gospel" against them.

Before we pass on from this chapter in St. Paul's life, written by himself, we should compare it narrowly with the historical narrative which runs parallel with it in the Acts. The passage before us is history at first hand, history written by the actor himself. The narrative in the Acts is history in the more ordinary sense of the word; it is the history of research, the history compiled from documents or from hearsay. The comparison of passages in the Bible which cover the same ground — and such passages seem purposely numerous and important—should enable us to determine accurately what is to be understood by an "inspired" history, and especially what kinds of authenticity and correctness are to be looked for in such history.

We may observe at once that, while there is of course no contradiction between St. Paul's own account and the narrative in the Acts, the colour given to the events is in the two cases so different, the connection and filling up of the outlines are so shifted, that if we had only the one source we should have been left quite in the dark upon several important points. We may also enter the plea that the personal narrative of St. Paul must be taken as the guiding clue by which the secondary narrative in the Acts is to be interpreted.

The three varying accounts of the conversion contained in Acts ix. 1–19, xxii. 3–16, xxvi. 12–18, are briefly summed up by the apostle in one pregnant phrase, "it pleased God to reveal His Son in me that I might preach Him among the Gentiles" (i. 16). He is writing of an event which happened some twenty years ago; the different details which survived in the tradition, whether those with him saw or did not see, heard or did not hear, how much was said on the road, how much in the house of Ananias—all these details which Paul alone could have satisfactorily explained and reconciled he passes over in silence. The one luminous, distinct, and memorable circumstance was precisely that "revelation of Jesus" in his own spirit, which every man who has come suddenly from unfaith to faith in Christ has experienced. The man's own account of his conversion is always the more instructive, while the popular version of it is usually the more entertaining.

After the conversion, it would seem from Acts ix. that the apostle remained "certain days" in Damascus, and then "when many days were fulfilled" went up to Jerusalem. From Acts xxii. 17 it would seem that he went to Jerusalem after an even shorter interval than "many days;" from Acts xxvi. 20 it would seem that a ministry in Damascus and in Jerusalem followed immediately upon the heavenly vision." Turning however to the autobiography, we find that after the conversion " neither went he up to Jerusalem to them who were apostles before him : but he went away into Arabia, and again he returned into Damascus ; then *after three years* he went up to Jerusalem to visit Cephas" (i. 17, 18). This is what we may call a different complexion given to the events, and it throws much light on the degree of accuracy, the minuteness of accuracy that we are to expect in the narratives and the reported speeches in the Acts. Again looking to Acts ix. 26–30, we should gather that the first visit to Jerusalem had been a very public and even notorious one ; "brought to the apostles, he was with them going in and going out at Jerusalem, preaching boldly in the name of the Lord," and when his boldness in disputation with the Hellenistic Jews had imperilled his life, he was despatched by the brethren to Tarsus by ship from Cæsarea. Certainly a different colour seems given to the visit when Paul tells us himself (Gal. i. 18, 19) that he was only in Jerusalem fifteen days, and saw only two of the apostles, Peter and James; that then he went to the country of which Tarsus was the capital, and was still unknown by face unto the Churches of Judæa. This last statement suggests that the verse, Acts xxvi. 20 ("throughout all the coasts of Judæa"), must refer to a much later period than it appears to do. Paul was fetched from his retirement at Tarsus by Barnabas (Acts xi. 25), and shortly afterwards he went to Jerusalem with his companion carrying alms. This visit he does not refer to in the letter, but he passes on to describe an important visit "after the space of fourteen years" (Gal. ii. 1–10). This would seem to be the visit described in Acts xv., the visit which resulted in what has sometimes unwisely been called the Council of Jerusalem. If these two passages are parallel accounts of the same event, we certainly have a most instructive light thrown upon what may be termed the freedom of inspired narrative. In the Acts we read that Paul is sent up to Jerusalem as a deputation to the apostles by the Church of Antioch. It would seem that the mission is open and public, and in deference to the demand of the Syrian Christians an assembly of apostles and elders is gathered together. Paul himself gives a different version of the mission: he went up, he says, "by revelation," and he laid the great question of Jewish Christianity which agitated the Church, not before the large assembly, " but privately before them who were of repute." The formal decree of a kind of Ecumenical Council promulgated for the benefit of many churches, enjoining abstinence "from things sacrificed to idols and from blood and from things strangled and from fornication" dwindles in St. Paul's own narrative to a very informal, but very hearty recognition of the Gentile ministry, with a general injunction that the Gentile party "should remember the poor." Reconciliation between these two versions of Paul's famous visit to Jerusalem taxes the ingenuity of Harmonists. If what we have called the cast-iron theory of inspiration is to be applied, we are certainly landed in a strange difficulty ; either we must say the two narratives do not apply to the same event, which makes a history of St. Paul's life well-nigh impossible, or we must conclude that the writers are not in harmony, and therefore on the cast-iron theory not *inspired*. But if we are following the Inductive method of determining what inspiration is, we shall reverently and scientifically record that the *inspired* Book may contain a history which is compiled subsequently to the events, and which therefore presents them in the form into which historical tradition has shaped them, and that occasionally the *inspired* book will give us an original document which rectifies the trifling deviations of historical tradition, and thereby teaches us not to found our faith upon a theory of guaranteed accuracy in historical details.

But now to leave this passage of history, we find ourselves at once plunged into the apostle's fiery vindication of the freedom of his gospel, and of its spiritual independence of Judaism, out of which it seemed to spring. The argument is bold even to the verge of exaggeration; indeed if the Epistle stood alone, if it were not supplemented by the calmer, fuller and more genial Epistle to the Romans, we might easily misunderstand this vehement contention. The startling assertion is made that the Law of Moses, that venerated code on which the Jewish faith seemed to rest, is to be regarded as a kind of episode, almost a retrogressive episode, in the history of religion. The apostle reverts to the primitive religion of Abraham, and claims for it a continuity with the gospel he had preached to the Galatians. "The blessing of Abraham," the doctrine that the Righteous shall live by faith, is come upon the Gentiles in Christ Jesus, and it would seem as if the history of the Law and its ordinances might be ignored. The glorious message of Christ, the religion of the Spirit, is set in striking contrast over against the Law. It is the boast of the apostle, who had himself been brought up under the Law, that through the law he has died unto the law that he might live unto God (ii. 19). The Law is not of faith, he says, and it was Christ's great service to deliver us from the curse of the Law (iii. 13), "to redeem them which were under the law that they might receive the adoption of sons" (iv. 5). At the best the sacred Law can only be regarded as the slave whose duty it was to take the child from his home to the school, the tutor to lead us to Christ; "now faith is come we are no longer under a tutor" (iii. 25). The sacred ordinances are treated only as "elements of the world" (iv. 3) hardly distinguishable from the rites of heathendom (iv. 8). The holy days enjoined by the Law, Sabbaths, New Moons, day of atonement, &c. (see Col. ii. 16), are treated almost as marks of spiritual declension (iv. 10), and the sacred rite, ordained by God, the mark of the chosen people, imposed on Christ Himself, and never by Him repudiated, is condemned as inconsistent with the gospel (v. 2), is treated as a mere mark of respectability, a concession in order to escape persecution (vi. 12), while he even allows himself a kind of broad sarcasm in denouncing those who insist on its observance (v. 12). Under this fiery invective all the outworks of Judaism crumbled away. Peter himself, "drawing back and separating himself, fearing them that were of the circumcision" (ii. 12), becomes an object deserving of chastisement; and with Peter, all the Jewish apostles and elders who like James wished to make Judaism a prerequisite of Christianity, were routed and dispersed. In place of a Christianized Judaism, the wonderful gospel of the Spirit is revealed clear cut and distinct from the old religion. "God sent forth the Spirit of His Son into our hearts, crying Abba, Father" (iv. 6). "Walk by the Spirit ... if ye are led by the Spirit, ye are not under the Law" (v. 16). Dead to the Law are those who have been crucified with Christ (ii. 20). "If we live by the Spirit, by the Spirit let us walk" (v. 25). Over against the Law and its bondage stands the Spirit in its freedom. Over against a Judaism which accepts Christ as only the greatest of the prophets stands Christianity itself. Over against the cramping organization in which men delight, with rites and symbols and observances of times and seasons, stands the grandly simple and expansive life of the Son of God, and of those who have entered into His sonship.

Here was a contention which did not apply to the Churches of Galatia alone; it applies to the Churches of all time. There was a danger, arising from the circumstances of the case, that the religion of Jesus should be presented as a national and not as an universal religion. The Lord Himself had lived as a Jew; He Himself had declared that He had come to fulfil the Law, and not to abolish it. "The scribes and Pharisees sit in Moses' seat; all therefore that they command you to do, do ye" (Matt. xxiii. 2). "I was not sent but unto the lost sheep of the house of Israel" (Matt. xv. 24). The immediate followers of Jesus were apt to misunderstand these sayings. The Religion of the Temple was still standing; its sacrifices and ordinances were in full operation. James, the head of the Church at Jerusalem, was famous, and even wins the approbation of Josephus, for his strict observation of the Law. His knees were "hard like a camel's" with kneeling upon the Temple marbles. The powerful church organization of Judaism was as yet unimpaired; and Christians of the type of James would seek to introduce Christ and His doctrine into the existing organization. The new wine was to be put into the old bottles; and the Jewish followers of Christ seemed hardly aware that the Lord had Himself warned them against that error; had Himself predicted the destruction of the Holy Temple and the Holy City as the beginning of the Kingdom of God. It was Paul who was raised up as the Divine agent to counteract this tendency and to elicit the Universalistic elements in the teaching of Jesus. It was his teaching, the earliest distinct record of which lies in the Epistle before us, which secured once and for ever the freedom and the spirituality of the Gospel of Christ. Standing aside from the apostolic succession, and resisting Peter to the face, he is the great inspired forerunner of those who in all ages have vindicated the direct revealing power of the Spirit of God, the independence of organizations and externals, which marks off "his gospel" from all the religions of the world. It was Paul's peculiar advantage to be a contemporary of Jesus, and in that sense to be a witness of the human life, and yet never to have known "Christ after the flesh." In direct and startling manifestation to his spirit the crucified Jesus had made Himself known, and in a manner which, as St. Paul himself would say, can be known only to spiritual minds, had revealed His person, His work, and His will. The strong insistence which St. Paul always lays upon the crucifixion and the resurrection reminds us continually that he is preaching the same Jesus of Nazareth that the ordained Twelve were preaching; but otherwise He has no time to touch upon the sweet familiar records of the earthly life: in his letters, at any rate, he does not refer to parable or miracle or precept as the ground-work of his gospel; but always contemplating his Lord as He is in His eternal nature, and His Lord's work as it takes its place in the great chain of the Divine dealings with the world, he is able, as the other apostles never were, to bring man at once to the centre, the pith of the revelation of God, and to preach Christ crucified as the means of salvation for the world.

Out of the polemic, then, against those obscure disturbers of the obscure Galatian churches grew a doctrine and a principle of permanent significance. Stand for a moment outside the historical circumstances of the letter, and the words speak to us as if they were addressed to us for the first time. The tendency to rest in elaborate organization, or in ancient forms, in the *opera operata* of ecclesiasticism, stands rebuked; and the practical bearings of a free Spiritual religion, depending *immediately* and moment by moment upon an actual and present Spirit of God, and upon a sonship to God secured by the Spirit, are permanently explained. The works of the flesh, the results of a Law which attempts to work from the outside inwards, are stated, and we are forewarned. On the other hand, the beautiful fruits of the Spirit are shown to result from the religion of the Spirit (v. 16). The Judaizers are always with us, as are also the Galatians, ready to be moved by them from the hope of the gospel. But, thank God, Paul with his burning argument, and better still the Eternal Spirit, by whom we are commanded to walk and to live, is always with us also.

Now when we come to consider the place which this teaching of St. Paul takes in the development of religion, we shall not be in much doubt concerning the meaning of inspiration as applied to such a work. Our inquiry, so far as it has proceeded, should place the *inspiration* of the Epistle that we have examined on an unassailable height. When we demand something more than we have found we are dominated by an *à priori* conception of what inspiration ought to be; when we accept and understand what we have found we are, or ought to be, very well satisfied with the inspiration which is perceptible in the Letter. So clear and indubitable does this quality, this note which we call the note of inspiration, appear, that we may proceed to notice some of the human elements which are discernible in the composition and the argument without in the least endangering our firmly established conviction. An inspired writing reminds one of a fabric of cloth of gold, which reflects the light of Heaven, and renders to the patient observer the unmistakable design which is wrought on it; but when the warp and the weft are more carefully examined, the strands into which the design is worked are seen to be anything but gold. It is simply blinding our eyes to the facts, and endangering our honesty of judgment, not to recognize the human and limited elements even in an inspired writer like St. Paul. If our public teachers have feared to point them out, it has been because the expressed or the implicit theory of inspiration seemed to be imperilled by their recognition. That want of candour which is sometimes charged upon religious teachers, is not so much disingenuousness as timidity; it is thought better to maintain that a thing is Divine and incomprehensible, even when to the unbiased judgment it seems comprehensible and human, than to imperil the whole conception of Inspiration by declaring 'this or that is palpably and certainly a flaw or a weakness due to the fact that the writer was a man.' And no doubt our teachers were in the main right. They waited for a time when the advance of scholarship would demand and supply a conception of Inspiration which would not be shattered by the admission of obvious facts.

Let us look fearlessly at some of these human

limitations in this inspired writing before us; and if we emphasize them a little strongly it is only because we are now in a position to do so without raising the outcry that we are undermining inspiration. Astronomers who point out spots in the sun are not assaulting the orb of light; they are explaining it; they are enabling us to understand it.

Take, to begin with, the verse (iii. 16), " He saith not unto seeds as of many, but as of one; and to thy seed which is Christ." Turn to the passages from which this quotation is taken. They are Gen. xii. 7, " And the Lord appeared unto Abram and said, Unto thy seed will I give this land," and Gen. xvii. 7, " And I will establish my covenant between me and thee and thy seed after thee throughout all generations for an everlasting covenant, to be a God unto thee and to thy seed after thee." Now when St. Paul lays stress on the collective noun *seed*, and argues that the promise pointed to Christ because it did not use the plural *seeds*, we may say without disrespect that he is showing a trace of his Rabbinical training.[1] Reasoning of that kind, such splitting of hairs, was intelligible in the Rabbinical Schools. Perhaps there has never been a group of intelligent men

---

[1] My friend Canon Driver informs me that the Hebrew word of which *seeds* is a translation, was used by the late Jews to signify " successive generations." This, as Canon Driver says, if it does not render the argument forcible, at least makes it a fair *argumentum ad hominem.*

besides to whom it would be intelligible. The Rabbinical Halachôth would furnish many examples of such reasoning, but it is sufficiently plain that the passages in Genesis leave no room to imagine that they contemplated the one person Christ, or if they did they could not have meant to express it by using *seed* instead of *seeds*, for *seeds* in such a connection would have been absolutely unmeaning. Rightly considered, this trace of the school of Gamaliel in the thought of the great apostle will be deeply instructive; it reminds us of the miracle which was wrought by the Divine Spirit when Saul the Jew and the Pharisee became the teacher of the Gospel of the Gentiles.

Take another instance of the same kind of limitation, imposed this time not by the apostle's training, but by the tradition of the Elders. In iii. 19 it is said that the law was ordained 'through angels.' In the Pentateuch we find no notice of the kind; but in the Septuagint the last clause of Deut. xxxiii. 2, in the blessing of Moses reads, "at his right hand *angels were with Him*." It would appear therefore that the apostle gives us here a glimpse into those innumerable traditional embellishments of the Pentateuch which at last quite overweighted the original Law. We need not say that the Law was not 'ordained through angels,' but we may say that such a statement cannot be maintained from this passage, which is merely a quotation from the traditional lore of the schools. While we are looking at verse 19 we may cast a glance at verse 20. It is said that 430 interpretations of this obscure verse have been suggested! Nor can we say that any of them has given us the writer's true meaning. And if it were not presumptuous to hazard another explanation, perhaps it might be suggested that the apostle in the rush and the fervour of his argument simply left his idea *unexpressed.* Perhaps a day will come when it will seem to earnest men less injurious to the Divine Scriptures to admit such a possibility, than to maintain that a verse is an oracle of God which is susceptible of 430 different meanings, none of which is at all satisfactory. Such a want of lucidity it may be less dangerous to charge upon St. Paul than on the Spirit of God.

Finally, let us look at the remarkable passage iv. 21–31, in which the apostle tries to prove from the Law for the sake of those who wish to be under the Law, that the Law is insufficient. To accomplish this he takes the history of Hagar and Ishmael, and would have us believe that these stand for Israel, while Isaac, from whom, be it observed, the Israelites actually derived their descent, stands for the genuine believers in Christ. These postulates granted, the demonstration proceeds with considerable force. Sinai is Hagar, the new Jerusalem is the seed of faith, the spiritual children; certainly on this understanding the Law gives a clear account of the Judaizers persecuting spiritually-minded Christians. But Luther surely puts it very mildly when he says "as a proof it is too weak to stand the test." Some would be inclined to say that as an illustration even it is singularly confusing; and believers in the Law who were convinced by such an argument that their own Law condemned them, and that the command "cast out the handmaid and her son" was actually meant to apply to them, would not have been very formidable opponents; they would hardly have required such a powerful weapon as this Epistle to overthrow them. In this illustration again we see reflected the methods which the Jewish interpreters adopted in using the Old Testament. By such methods one need not despair of proving anything from any passage. And the only consideration which may throw some light on the apostle's argument here is that possibly the Judaizing party, accustomed to reasoning of the kind, were able to see in this instance a cogency which entirely escapes our observation. Some colour to this supposition is afforded by St. Paul's undoubted habit of first establishing his doctrine upon broad spiritual grounds, and then supporting it, apparently with his eye upon Jewish readers, by quotations from the ancient Scriptures, which possibly they might accept in the sense he intended, but which to us appear to have little relevancy. If we have given a disproportionate importance to these human strands in the warp and woof of our cloth of gold, it has been rendered necessary by the strange timidity which is often displayed in dealing with the subject. But in summing up the conclusions of this chapter we may allow these facts which have been last considered to fall into their proper place, and it surely is a sufficiently insignificant one.

We have found that the Epistle to the Galatians is an intensely energetic work from the pen of a man who, more than any other, caught and understood the Universal aspects of Christ's religion; we have found that the work was elicited by the special circumstances of the Galatian Christians; but those circumstances, while special, were typical, and are constantly recurring, so that the argument and the teaching have a permanent significance. We have found that the writer in his vindication of his personal independence, and of his direct spiritual ordination from on high, not only repudiated any subordination to those who were apostles before him, but also gave to the events which were current in the apostolic tradition a certain variation of colour, which makes it difficult to reconcile the Acts with the Epistle; but in the overwhelmingly convincing reality and trustworthiness of the autobiographical passage we have found a standard and regulator for the interpretation of that early history. Lastly, we have found traces of the writer's rabbinical training and rabbinical habits of thought; but in proportion as these have been forced upon our attention we have been the more filled with astonishment that one coming from such a school should have been the means of widening the Gospel Message to embrace the world, and of discovering its permanent basis in the deep facts of the Spirit. It is thus apparent that the Letter of the Inspired Book does not cease to be a human production; on the contrary, it is suggested by incidental circumstances, and it is written by a man who is not raised above his human lot, but is of like passions with ourselves. But it is equally apparent that the Letter of the Inspired Book is quite unlike any other letters that have ever been written; it is suggested by circumstances which occur in the progress of God's revelation to men; it is written by one in whom God "has revealed His Son," and consequently it teems with knowledge which can only be gained from the Spirit of God, and it presents ideas which have not their genesis in the character or the training of the writer, and which can only be explained by referring them to the Eternal Mind itself. While, therefore, our examination of this Epistle has clarified, it is not likely to have lowered, our idea of what is meant by inspiration.

Before we turn from this branch of the subject, we may just remind ourselves that we have at most only taken a specimen for examination. The three other unquestioned letters of the apostle are even more fruitful than that to the Galatians in lofty argument and inspired dealing with ethical questions. The two Epistles to the Thessalonians, and those to Philemon and the Philippians, are much lighter, but they repay the closer study quite as well. The two very similar treatises to the Ephesians and the Colossians, though suggesting some difficulties from the standpoint of the higher criticism, are rich in pregnant thought concerning the Person of Christ and the Community of which He is the Head; in studying them the student's trouble does not consist in finding the *inspiration*—that is very obvious —but in clearing his mind of the prejudice that the inspiration depends upon their Pauline authorship. The three Pastoral Epistles do not rank with those which have been already mentioned, they touch chiefly upon questions of external organization, in which it is difficult to trace the breath of inspiration; but as giving the earliest and the eternally essential directions for the ordering of Christian communities, they have a place in the " writings which are profitable." The New Testament would be incomplete without them.

The Letter of the Inspired Book is not confined to St. Paul's writings. There is the Epistle to the Hebrews; there are the so-called Catholic Epistles, by which we are to understand treatises not addressed to any particular community, but to the Church at large. Into these we need not enter just at present. When the principles of treatment which we have been employing have been to some extent mastered, these minor writings of the New Testament present comparatively little difficulty. Just to give one example in bringing this chapter to a close, the Epistle of James stands as the most marked survival in the Canon of that Jewish side of Christianity, the dangers of which St. Paul clearly perceived. It is not difficult to quote from the Epistle sentences which seem meant as direct contradictions of St. Paul's doctrine (compare James ii. 21, with Rom. iv. 2, 3), but only a very artificial theory of inspiration will make a difficulty out of this; the writer of the Judaist Epistle did not grasp the truth of Christ quite as Paul did. To try and show that they *agree*, is to frustrate one great purpose of the Inspired Book, the object of which is not to give a complete account of Paul's Christianity or of James's Christianity, but to reflect fully the different aspects of the truth which affect different minds. From this point of view the antinomies of the New Testament are a confirmation rather than a weakening of its claim.

CHAPTER III.

ON THE BIOGRAPHIES OF THE INSPIRED BOOK.

BIOGRAPHICAL sketches play a considerable part in the Old Testament. We have a fairly complete biography of Samuel in the book called by his name. We have the materials for a tolerably full life of David. A fragment of biography from the traditions of the schools of the prophets gives us a glimpse into the life of Elijah. And so on. But these biographies occur rather in the way of episodes; they can scarcely be said to have a significance as biographies. It is far otherwise with the biographies of the New Testament. The dual biography which recounts and tacitly compares the lives of Peter and Paul, the Acts of the Apostles as we call it, is no episode. The lives of those two remarkable men exhibit the life of the apostolic church; in them the two tendencies which the new faith contained within it, the Judaistic tendency and the tendency to break down the barriers of race and to bring the Jew and Gentile into a common fold—these two tendencies are shown running parallel and in spite of all opposing difficulties actually blending with one another. Biography in such a case is not merely the lives of representative men; it is the history of a movement, of a growth, of a consummation, which found a complete expression in two remarkable personalities. But even this significance of the dual biography would not be reason enough for giving a chapter to the subject of biography. That reason is found in the unique place which the biography of Jesus holds in the biblical literature. The life of Jesus is no episode in the history of a people or a faith; it is the very core of both. If the biography were confined to one sentence, "Jesus being such an one as He was actually lived and died," we should immediately fix upon that statement as the pivot upon which the whole of the New Testament turns, the goal to which all the Old Testament moved. It is remarkable, for instance, that St. Paul hardly concerned himself with the life of Christ, he was so entirely occupied with the fact that he *had* lived and died. Look at it from before or from behind, the significance of that fact can hardly be evaded. Are we thinking of Judaism with its reaching out towards a cherished ideal? That life presents itself as the fulfilment of the Messianic hope, the satisfaction of all that the Law dimly desired and the prophets vaguely foretold. Or are we looking back upon the spiritual influence which has worked so potently in the world during the Christian centuries, is working so potently still, and promises to work so much more potently in the future? Then we trace this astonishing influence back to that life, and if we knew nothing at all about it, but had to construct it out of the creative imagination, we should have to figure to ourselves facts, sayings, and impressions which would account for what has flowed from it. Thus if the place where this biography comes were actually a blank, we should be able to surmise something of what ought to be there, just as astronomers surmised the existence of a new planet, and knew in what quarter of the heavens to look for it, by observing and registering the influences which retarded or deflected the movements of the other planets.

Or to put it in another way, the life of Christ might be in its place as the pivot of Christianity and the goal of Judaism, and yet be only a veiled figure, the fashion and even the outlines of which should remain for ever beyond our searching.

From this broad view of the question we are able to appreciate the position which the Life of Christ holds in the Inspired Book, and we ought also to be prepared for the very singular phenomena which the records of the Life actually present.

When we speak of Inspired Writings, we should take the biography of Jesus as the typical Inspired Writing. So sacred, so inspired, has the *Evangelium*, just as it stands, appeared to the Christian consciousness, that already in the second century the existence of four distinct narratives appeared as essential and significant as the existence of the four cardinal points of the compass. All of us who have any faith in inspiration at all would be inclined to say, " Well, let this writing or that be considered inspired, as you please, but beyond all manner of question these Gospels are inspired." There will be such an universal agreement on this point, this particular section of the Bible, as the best known and the most frequently read, will be so naturally in the minds of all when the question of Inspiration is raised, that it furnishes a peculiarly useful and interesting subject for the illustration of our inquiry. Here, at any rate, is an inspired writing, an inspired writing which we are all agreed to call inspired. We may freely look the facts in the face, therefore, without being supposed to be undermining the belief in inspiration; we freely look the facts in the face not in order to undermine, but to determine, the belief in inspiration. Whether it is a matter of tradition and authority, or a matter of impression, or, as we sometimes put it, internal evidence, matters very little for the purpose that is now in hand. The writing is inspired. Whatever facts may emerge in the inquiry, however little they may accord with a previously conceived theory of inspiration, none the less the writing is inspired. And here, as elsewhere in the inquiry which we are trying to conduct, our business is to master the facts in order that we may know fully and state clearly what we are to mean, and what we are not to mean, by an inspired book. In the matter of the Gospels more than anywhere else, a preconceived theory of what inspiration ought to be is absolutely fatal. It is the source of endless unveracity, and the source, amongst other things, of that very questionable labour which occupies and baffles the the wits of Harmonists.

Now we can hardly question that if we had formed *à priori* an idea of what a biography of our Lord ought to be, we should have pictured to ourselves a single narrative, detailed and complete, with every event in the life arranged in a chronological order, every miracle rightly placed in time and circumstance, every utterance fully and accurately set down without possibility of question that the very words He used were recorded precisely as He used them. Perhaps our *à priori* idea would also have included a careful explanation of how the pre-existent life passed into the earthly life, of how the Divine consciousness harmonized with the human nature, and of how the offering on the Cross accomplished the salvation of the world. The efforts which have been made for many ages to settle these and similar questions from the gospel narratives, however unavailing they may be, show at least what kind of a biography we should have had written if we had been asked to lay down the conditions of an inspired writing.

Or if we had so far seen the advantage of a quadruple narrative as to admit its necessity, our *à priori* idea would have at least demanded that the four narratives should strikingly harmonize, and that in no single point should there be the slightest discrepancy between their several versions of the same events. And if we had admitted the desirability of having the four Gospels, we should certainly have required that each of them should have a clearly ascertainable origin and authorship; we should expect each writer not only to give his name, but to mention when he was writing and to show how he derived his information, and to give proof that the information so derived was authentic or even divinely guaranteed against all possibility of error.

No doubt there are other points which individual believers would have insisted on if they had been consulted; but the conditions just enumerated would have been declared with unanimous consent to be essential. And so powerful is the influence of a preconceived theory in such a matter as Inspiration, that many people have actually convinced themselves that the conditions their theory demanded are fulfilled in the Gospel narrative; and, growing hot in the maintenance of their dogma, they will sometimes try to charge it as a heresy on honest men when the facts which run counter to their dogma are pointed out. We must be careful not to treat a simple appeal to facts as an attack on Inspiration. Such an appeal is not an attack upon Inspiration, but only the refutation of a wrong theory of Inspiration, of a theory which is dogmatic and violent just in proportion as it suspects in calmer moments its own baselessness. When we fear that we are unable to give a reason of the faith which is in us, we naturally regard any one who asks us for a reason as an assailant of our faith. The irascibility of dogmatists is sometimes due to this simple law.

Turning now from what we should expect Inspired Biography to be, we come to what Inspired Biography is. There are four narratives instead of one. There are parts of the ground common to all four, where we are able to test the degree of accuracy which we are to look for in the narrative by seeing how far they diverge from one another in the treatment of the same facts. Then there are features in each narrative which do not appear in any of the other three. The four narratives, in a word, overlap to a greater or lesser extent, but the borders in no case exactly coincide.

We say there are four narratives, but when we examine the material a little more closely we have to modify the statement. It is more correct to say that there are two narratives, one of which comes to us in a triple form, one of which stands quite by itself. The explanation of this curious phenomenon must be deferred until we have examined the facts with some minuteness. We shall secure clearness in our inquiry if we endeavour first to get an idea of the nature of the Triple narrative, then to look at the Single narrative, and afterwards to compare the two together.

What is this Triple narrative which is usually called by the names of Matthew and Mark and Luke? Each of the three versions has special characteristics, characteristics which have led commentators to make a great many conjectures; for instance, they tell us that Matthew is written for Jews, because one mark of this Gospel is its quotation of Old Testament prophecy. Then they tell us that Mark is more graphic in detail than the others, and more disposed to dwell upon the transactions of the life, as distinct from the teaching, of the Lord. Again, they tell us that Luke is written for Gentiles, because it bears the stamp of the Greek touch upon it. This is all conjecture, very interesting conjecture, but it is not very fruitful conjecture, because it always remains as a question in the background why should inspired biography have to be retold for different groups of hearers, and if for Jews and for Greeks, why not also for the other tribes of flesh and blood which were afterwards to come and inquire concerning the matchless life? On the whole, possibly traditionalism has been blinding our eyes and leading us into somewhat unremunerative inquiries. Instead of beginning with the peculiarities of the several narratives, it would seem more natural to begin with what is common to the three. And when once we are started upon that investigation, we are quickly rewarded with most interesting discoveries. In fact, it appears that, notwithstanding the considerable differences of treatment, there is running through all three narratives a line of narrative which is almost verbally identical in each. Just to test this statement, let us take a paragraph where the three Gospels run together, and, leaving out what is peculiar, let us write down what is common, merely throwing in between brackets connecting words from one or the other, where the purely grammatical divergences prevent the sentences from accurately fitting. Suppose we take the passage which begins in Mark i. 40, and runs parallel with Matthew viii., ix., and with Luke v. 12–39. Here is the common thread running through all. ["There came a] leper saying [unto] him, If thou wilt thou canst make me clean. And he stretched forth his hand, and touched him, [and] saith, I will, be thou made clean. And straightway the leprosy [departed from] him. And [he saith] unto him, Say [nothing] to any man, but shew thyself to the priest and offer [what] Moses commanded for a testimony unto them. And [they come] bringing [one] sick of the palsy. And [Jesus] seeing their faith [saith] Thy sins are forgiven. [The] Scribes [say] This [man] blasphemeth. Jesus [saith] Why [reason] in your hearts? Whether is easier to say Thy sins are forgiven, or to say Arise? But that ye may know that the son of man hath power on earth to forgive sins,—to the [sick of the] palsy,— Arise, take up thy [bed] and [go] into thy house; and [he] went, and glorified God. And [he saw Levi] sitting at the place of toll, and [saith] unto him, Follow me. And he arose and followed him.

And in [the] house many publicans sat. And the Pharisees said [unto] His disciples, He eateth with publicans and sinners. [Jesus said] They that are strong have no need of a physician, but they that are sick; I came not to call the righteous, but sinners. John's disciples [come and say unto] him, The Pharisees fast, but thy [disciples do not]. Jesus said [unto] them, Can the sons of the bride-chamber, [while] the bridegroom is with them? But the days will come when the bridegroom shall be taken away from them, then will they fast. No man [seweth] a piece on an old garment. No [man] putteth new wine into old wineskins, else burst the skins and [the wine] perisheth, and the skins; but [they put] new wine into fresh bottles. Going [on the] Sabbath through cornfields his disciples pluck ears of corn. [The] Pharisees [say Why] do [that] which is not lawful [on the] Sabbath? [He said] to them, Did ye read [what] David did [when] he was an hungred, and they that were with him? He entered into the house of God and did eat the shewbread, which it [is] not lawful to eat save [for] the priests. [And gave] to them [that were with] him. [And he] said, The Son of Man is Lord of the Sabbath."

If we consider closely the passage just quoted, we cannot but be struck with the resemblance it all bears to the jottings of speeches which a reporter might make, intending to work up his notes afterwards. It will be noted that the common thread of narrative is marked even more by identity of language than by identity of thought. But if you get three people to report an event or a speech immediately afterwards, you will see at once that the identity of thought is far more striking than the identity of language. It may even happen that while all three give substantially the same account, there will be hardly any points of verbal connection at all. Taking this into account, we can hardly doubt that this Triple Narrative is to be explained either by all three writers having before them a common source, or by their having seen each other's work. Look for a moment at the first hypothesis. No doubt from the earliest days there existed a carefully preserved record of the Lord's doings and sayings which passed from hand to hand, possibly even only from mouth to mouth, with as minute a verbal accuracy as the poems of Homer were learnt and taught before the invention of writing. It would seem probable that the expectation of the Lord's immediate return "in the clouds of heaven" might prevent any believer from attempting or demanding a written record. In that case, it would only be when the ruin of Jersualem had come, and the generation to which Jesus belonged was passing away without the expected advent of the Lord being realized, that the remaining followers of Christ who had seen and heard Him would feel the necessity of writing down what was so familiar to them for those who should come after. That gospels of this kind, all we may presume embodying the common thread and each adding more or less that was fresh according to circumstances, were composed in considerable numbers is shown by the preface to our third Gospel, which says, " Many have taken in hand to draw up a narrative concerning those matters which have been fulfilled among us, even as they delivered them unto us, which from the beginning were eye-witnesses and ministers of the word." This statement seems to throw a clear light on the composition of those early gospels, and to explain to some extent the striking phenomena which we have just examined in the three that have survived. But while the hypothesis of a common tradition in the Three Gospels explains some of the facts, it does not explain them all. When the three narratives are placed side by side in columns and carefully examined, it quickly appears that the relation between Matthew and Luke is much less close than that between Matthew and Mark, or than that between Luke and Mark. As the inquiry proceeds, in following the parallel columns, for instance, which Mr. Rushbrooke has compiled with such admirable care and skill, it becomes almost demonstrable that the narrative of Mark, in these passages where the three agree, was before Matthew and Luke, who made use of it each in his own way. A detailed proof of this would lead us too far afield. We must be content therefore simply to note the fact that our Gospels are historical narratives compiled by reference to existing sources, and that, singularly enough, side by side with two more elaborate narratives there has come to us one of the sources which both of them used. A careful study of Matthew and Luke reveals another strain of narrative which is common to them both, and seems to point to another source, possibly a collection of the Sayings of our Lord, just as Mark is a collection of His doings, which both of the evangelists brought into requisition.

When once we get some insight into the methods of compilation in the early times we can understand those divergences which occur in our three narratives, divergences which have occasioned much exultation to the assailants and suggested many attempts at harmonizing to the defenders of the Gospels. Both attack and defence are quite unnecessary, and arise entirely from a preconceived theory of what inspired biography ought to be. Only remember that Mark wrote before the others, embodying in his narrative a certain group of the memoirs of Jesus; that Matthew had the advantage of this work and also of another similar collection, besides being in possession of other materials which cannot be definitely traced; and that Luke had Mark's work and the other collection which Matthew employed, not to mention many other lives or memoirs of Jesus; and considering the variety of material, and the uncertainty that must have prevailed about many points of detail, we cannot be surprised that striking divergences occur, we can only be well content with the evidence which the divergences afford that we have

ON THE BIOGRAPHIES OF THE BIBLE. 69

to do with testimonies to the Life of our Lord which are to some extent independent of one another.

We are now prepared to look quite dispassionately at these divergences; let us take an instance from the opening pages of the Gospel.

Both the first and the third evangelists furnish us with pedigrees of the Lord Jesus Christ. It will be convenient to set these pedigrees down in parallel columns so far as they are on common ground (Matt. i. 2-16; Luke iii. 23-38).

MATTHEW:—	LUKE:—
Abraham	Abraham
Isaac	Isaac
Jacob	Jacob
Judah	Judah
Perez	Perez
Hezron	Hezron
Ram	Arni (or Aram)
Aminadab	Aminadab
Nahshon	Nahshon
Salmon	Salmon
Boaz	Boaz
Oved	Oved
Jesse	Jesse
David	David

So far the lists exactly tally, with the exception of the trifling change of Ram into Arni or Aram. Now let us continue the genealogy from David:—

MATTHEW:—	LUKE:—
David	David
Solomon	Nathan
Rehoboam	Mattahan
Abijah	Menna
Asa	Melea

MATTHEW:—	LUKE:—
Jehoshaphat	Eliakim
Joram	Jonam
Uzziah	Joseph
Jotham	Judas
Ahaz	Symeon
Hezekiah	Levi
Manasseh	Matthat
Amon	Jorim
Josiah	Eliezer
Jechoniah	Jesus
Shealtiel	Er
Zerubbabel	Elmadam
Abiud	Cosam
Eliakim	Addi
Azor	Melchi
Sadoc	Neri
Achim	*Shealtiel*
Eliud	*Zerubbabel*
Eleazar	Rhesa
Matthan	Joanan
Jacob	Joda
Joseph	Josech
Jesus	Semein
	Mattathias
	Maath
	Naggai
	Esli
	Nahum
	Amos
	Mattathias
	Joseph
	Jarmai
	Melchi
	Levi
	Matthat
	Heli
	Joseph
	Jesus

It is quite clear that the third Gospel has followed quite a different genealogical tree. The first Gospel presents a tempting symmetry; fourteen generations from Abraham to David; fourteen more from David to the Captivity; fourteen more from the Captivity to Jesus. In the third Gospel these last twenty-eight generations expand into thirty-eight, and not only so, but from David downwards the descent is drawn along different lines, which only show a momentary contact in the two first generations after the Captivity. So marked and irreconcilable is this difference, that even the father of Joseph is called Jacob in the one list, and Heli in the other. Here has been a fine field of labour for ingenious harmonists. A cast-iron theory of Inspiration required that the lists should coincide; and with really wonderful zeal the holders of the theory have wrought to bring these two different pedigrees to fit on to the same last. The most ingenious and poetical explanation deserves a passing notice because a coming generation of Bible students will find it almost incredible that such an explanation should have been seriously urged. It is said that one list is meant to be Joseph's pedigree and the other Mary's. Thus in coming down from King David, Joseph's family occupied twenty-eight generations, father and son, while in the same time Mary's family got through thirty-eight generations. This remarkable longevity of Joseph's ancestors, or this remarkable series of early deaths in Mary's family, is not felt to be a difficulty any more than the circumstance that Luke inadvertently states that Joseph was the son of Heli, when he meant Mary was the daughter of Heli.

The simple fact appears to be that the two writers had different genealogical lists before them, one of which may be correct, though it is hardly possible that both can be, and it is just conceivable that neither is. We may settle it therefore with ourselves that it is not inconsistent with inspired biography to include two different versions of such a thing as a pedigree. It may be said that the pedigree is a matter of slight importance. But there is no reason for shutting our eyes to the fact that divergences on matters of slight importance are admissible. We have the Gospels in our hands to see *what* they are, and to form our conception of inspiration accordingly. We may well be a little impatient with those who tell us, first that there are and can be no divergences, and when that is shown to be a mistake, exclaim, "But the divergences are in matters of slight importance."

We may, in passing, notice another divergence of slight importance which will serve as an illustration of what we may be prepared to expect. We never question that the early home of Jesus was at Nazareth. So undoubtedly it was, but our two authorities, the first and the third Gospels, give rather a different account of how it came to be His home. Luke (i. 26) shows us Joseph and Mary as citizens of that little city among the Galilean hills, who came up to Bethlehem only for the "taxing," because Bethlehem was the town to which they originally belonged. But the author of the first Gospel does not seem to have known that the two betrothed people were living in Nazareth to start with. Reading on from Matt. i. 18 to ii. 1, we should suppose that the parents were living at Bethlehem; and then at the end of the second chapter, Nazareth is mentioned for the first time in these words: "being warned of God in a dream, he (Joseph) withdrew into the parts of Galilee, *and came and dwelt in a city called Nazareth*, that it might be fulfilled which was spoken by the prophets that he should be called a Nazarene."

It is a very small matter no doubt, but does it not show us how mistaken we may be in demanding or in contending for a minute accuracy in the narrative of the Gospel? Does not the very existence of *four* narratives, instead of one, clearly presenting discrepancies of the kind we are now examining, serve as a warning against building *upon the letter?* Nor must it be supposed that these discrepancies are confined to those parts of the narrative which are of archaic rather than of practical importance. That we may not shirk the facts and blink the truth, let us examine for a moment a piece of the Lord's teaching as it is variously reported, and refer at any rate to one most momentous fact in the history where such divergences appear.

There is no utterance of our Lord's which breathes more richly and fully a divine fragrance than the Beatitudes recorded in Matt. v. 1–12. Read them through; they are fresh and living. This is the very atmosphere of the Kingdom of God. This conception of blessedness is so unlike what our own imaginations paint, so manifestly drawn from sources other than simple observation, that if we wanted a typical instance of Inspired speech we should be disposed to select this. To single out "the poor in spirit, them that mourn, the meek, those that hunger and thirst after righteousness, the merciful, the pure in heart, the peacemakers, those who are persecuted for righteousness' sake," and to treat them as the people who are to be congratulated, the true possessors not only of the Kingdom of Heaven, but also of the earth, the sons of God to whom belongs the beatific vision, the truly rejoicing and triumphant beings, happy under reproach and slander and persecution — this was a course which of itself might give Jesus the pre-eminence He holds amongst all who have ever sought to instruct the human race. It is therefore with a kind of pain that we find the Third Gospel recording instead of these wonderful beatitudes a balanced antithesis, three blessings accompanied by corresponding woes. In place of the sweetness and freshness and convincingness of the beatitudes, there is in this other version a certain hardness, an austerity, an incompleteness, which leaves us in doubt and perplexity. We may almost say that if we did not habitually interpret this formularized version by the light of the original and spontaneous version, we should find very little of the marks of the Lord Jesus in it. It says (Luke vi. 20), "Blessed are ye poor," not poor in spirit, but actually poor, and "woe unto you that are rich," implying that poverty is a title to the kingdom of heaven, and that a law of compensation will refuse to the rich any consolation hereafter. Again it says, "Blessed are ye that hunger now," not hunger after righteousness, but literally hunger, and "woe unto you that are full now," implying that asceticism is a title to blessedness, and that one who is blessed with plenty upon earth must be requited with hunger hereafter. And so with mourning. It is exalted as a good in itself; while laughter is condemned as an evil in itself; so that we can hardly detect in the speaker of these words the Son of man who "came eating and drinking," and whose earliest public appearance was at a marriage feast. Then the list closes with a kind of exaggerated statement of the original beatitude upon the persecuted for righteousness' sake, and a corresponding woe unto those of whom all men speak well.

Now of course it is open to us to say that these are two different discourses and both are literally reported. But as from our examination of the texture of our narratives we have been led to expect divergences of detail, it is altogether more natural to suppose that they are two reports of the same teaching, but that the second is not so good a report as the first, and has even received into itself a touch of the ascetic tinge which rapidly entered into the Church and finally issued in the excesses of the Anchorites: in fact it is better to do what has always instinctively been done, viz. to efface the second report under the first, or when we read the second to so interpret it by the first that we escape its peculiar quality and flavour.

We have to settle it with ourselves that inspired biography, coming to us in a triple form, may admit deviations even in matters of high importance, and may call for an earnest search, a spiritual search, in order to get behind the mere letter and realize the Person who lived and spoke, and the Spirit that lived and spoke in Him.

The momentous fact in the history above referred to which is marked by striking divergences is the Resurrection. This is just a case where the *à priori* theory of Inspiration would have demanded a single, straightforward, clear narrative of events. The fact of the resurrection being of primary importance, it being a Gospel of the Resurrection which was actually preached by the earliest preachers, it would seem quite essential that the narrative of the Resurrection should be placed upon exceptionally clear ground and supported by exceptionally cogent proofs. But no, the actual fact to be faced is that we have four accounts which tax, and may we not say defy, the utmost ingenuity of harmonists to weave them into a consistent whole. We seem to have recorded for us the broken, excited impressions which the fact made on the first witnesses, rather than the calm and judicial statement of the fact itself. And in this connection we may call attention to the curious divergence in the accounts of the Ascension which appear in the third Gospel and in the opening chapter of the Acts. If we had only the third Gospel we should suppose that immediately after the appearance of the Lord to the disciples on the evening of the day of the resurrection " he led them out until they were over against Bethany," and there " he was carried up into Heaven." And with this agrees Mark xvi. 19. In the opening chapter of the Acts this impression is corrected by an explicit statement that He had been " appearing unto them by the space of forty days, and speaking the things concerning the Kingdom of God," before He ascended into Heaven (cf. Matt. xxviii. 16–20). This is all the more noticeable, because, as is universally acknowledged, the author of the third Gospel is the author of the Acts; so that here we have a case of a writer correcting his own statement in the light of a fuller knowledge. Now certainly in this instance we are forced to a reverent admission that our presuppositions in the matter of Inspiration are very faulty and misleading. Instead of getting a simple single narrative of the

Resurrection and the Ascension, we have five separate narratives (not to mention St. Paul's summary of events in 1 Cor. xv., which does not seem to proceed on the lines of any of our Gospels); each narrative assures us of the fact of the Resurrection, and conveys, as it were, an impression of the wonder and the awe of it, but no two of them give the same sequence of events, and no one of them has ever been disturbed by the question whether this or that event will fit in with others elsewhere narrated; while the fact of the Ascension—if we except the vague notice of Mark xvi. 19—is related only by one of the authors, and he seems in his first treatise to have written in ignorance of the time at which it took place, and only in the second treatise to have realized that nearly six weeks elapsed between the Lord's rising from the tomb and His passing into the heavens. With this notable example before us, may we not say that the inspired biography labours with a kind of deliberate purpose to shatter the cast-iron theory of inspiration?

There is yet another point to be noticed in these three writings which embody the common narrative—a point which must necessarily surprise those who get their idea of Inspiration otherwise than from the facts—and that is, the writings are practically anonymous. It is true tradition has preserved titles for the books; it informs us that the first of them is "The glad tidings *according* to St. *Matthew*," the second is "The glad tidings *according to St. Mark*," and the third is "The glad tidings *according to St. Luke*." But the expression does not leave it beyond doubt that the actual composition is to be referred to men bearing these names. Suppose—and it is a very possible supposition—that Matthew the publican in his apostolic preaching had been accustomed to dwell on a certain cycle of facts, and to quote a certain number of the Lord's discourses; and suppose that at his wish, or even after his death, his immediate followers had carefully set down his evangelic teaching, the Writing so formed might very appropriately have been styled "The good news according to Matthew" (τὸ κατὰ Ματθαῖον ἅγιον εὐαγγέλιον). Even tradition then can hardly be said to speak very decisively on the question of the authorship. It is true on the other hand, that nothing need hinder us from accepting this tradition. We know nothing of Matthew except from the notices of the Gospels themselves, nothing of Mark and Luke except from the Acts and the Epistles; the traditional stories which cluster round their names for the most part only sprang out of the belief that they were the authors of the Gospels. From what we know of these men, we cannot say that there is any improbability in ascribing the Writings to them. But apart from this tradition, which is not very explicit and assuredly by no means authoritative, we may call the three Gospels anonymous. In the first one there is no hint throughout concerning the authorship. If Matthew, the disciple of Jesus, wrote it, then it is very worthy of remark that he carefully withheld his name, and scrupulously avoided laying any claim to credence on the ground that he had any special commission to write, or even on the ground that he had seen with his eyes or heard with his ears. Mark, to whom tradition ascribes the second Gospel, is equally reticent; there is no mention of his own name in the work, there is no statement of his claim to be believed. The author of the third Gospel, in his preface, steps forward a little more prominently as a writer; but here it is to be observed that he makes no pretence of any other qualification for writing than such as historians usually urge. " Having traced the course of all things accurately from the first," and having been in communication with eye-witnesses of the events, it seemed good unto him to write the biography. That is all he tells us about himself, all he tells us about his mission. It would seem then that in our estimate of these Gospels we are not to treat the authorship as an essential factor. The authors themselves implicitly forbid us to do so. We may go a little further. In describing the character and quality of their writings, we must not claim for them what they do not claim for themselves, and what no other writer in the New Testament claims for them. We must be exceedingly careful not to formulate a theory of Inspiration which would, for example, give the lie to the explicit statement of his method and qualifications made by Luke in the preface to his Gospel. And if we have not remained within these bounds which fact requires, and if in consequence divergences in the three narratives have been a great stumbling-block to us and have impelled us to desperate resorts in order to smooth away, or to hide them, then we must remember that at any rate these modest, self-repressing writers are not to blame; we cannot say that any of them led us to expect that in recording what he knew of the Lord's life and sayings he would be free from all possibility of error; we cannot say that any of them ever made those bombastic claims which have sometimes been made for them, claims which, in asserting that the Holy Ghost practically penned their writings, make every candid admission of discrepancy or error in them a blasphemous charge against the Holy Ghost. We have ourselves to blame for the misunderstanding of the Scriptures; we profess to pay them the most unbounded deference, and yet we seldom are content with the account they give of themselves, but must needs invent attributes for them by which we intend to honour them, but which, being our own invention, only bring dishonour upon them when the inevitable day of reckoning comes and the quiet truth irresistibly asserts itself.

But it is time now to turn to what we have called the Single Narrative, which lies side by side in our New Testament with the Triple Narrative just briefly examined. The Single Narrative is certainly very unlike the Triple Narrative. It sometimes records the same events, it sometimes seems to be recording even the same discourses; but there is a difference: it is, if we may use an image, the difference between Turner's pictures of Venice and Canaletto's; the main features are there; the atmosphere is different, the colouring is different. Jesus of Nazareth, we seem forced to admit, creates the impression which is recorded in the Triple Narrative. Jesus of Nazareth, we seem still more forced to admit, created the impression which is recorded in this Single Narrative. The difference seems to lie in a spiritual receptivity, a preparedness, a comprehension in the observer. Venice was to Canaletto what he in that dull eighteenth century successfully put upon canvas, and Venice was to Turner what he with his unique gift successfully put upon canvas. In the same way Jesus was to common observers the Jesus of the Triple Narrative, a lovely and gracious Being, blending tenderness and rigour, a Teacher speaking as never man spake before, a Power controlling the forces of nature, a martyr, dignified, pathetic, triumphant. But Jesus was also to certain others who " beheld his glory, glory as of the only begotten from the Father," all that and even more than appears in the Triple Narrative. All and even more, we say, because when the narrative closes, the writer seems to see the Subject of his biography growing before his eyes, and by a bold hyperbole he supposes that even the world itself could not contain the books which should be written if a full account were given. What a contrast is here! On the one hand is the Triple Narrative, calm, objective, self-contained, naïve and simple, recording the appearance without much sense of embarrassment. On the other hand is this Single Narrative, rapt, subjective, contemplative, expansive, simple too in its way, but with an undertone of trouble, a questioning whether the world can ever believe the wonderful things which it has to tell concerning what certain men had heard and seen with their eyes and their hands had handled.

It would seem, then, that the way of Inspired Biography was to give us two versions of its Subject; the one fragmentary, irregular, almost, one may say, haphazard, and yet unspeakably attractive, direct and human, freed from all unnecessary mystery; the other methodical, complete, developed on a definite plan, but deeper, appealing to an awakened spiritual sense, dealing with mystery, giving also the clue to mystery, just because the human spirit itself in all its higher phases must always enter the cloud. If we recognize this broad and certainly very unexpected phenomenon of the Inspired Biography we shall be able with an unblenched face to look into the facts which are connected with it.

It may be observed at once that the Single Narrative not only comes a good way after the other, but we may almost say that it consciously revised and corrected it. We cannot tell whether the writer had the actual Gospels which we now possess before him, but one thing seems plain: he was very familiar with the body of tradition which actually finds expression in our Triple Narrative, and where in his fuller and complete knowledge he knew that tradition to be correct, he was content to be silent; where, on the other hand, he knew there were slight errors, he corrected them; but his main purpose was to give a side of the Lord's life which, from the very nature of the case, could have found no place in the common tradition. To make this assertion definite by illustration: the Communion of the Supper was so universally known and observed when he wrote, that he actually does not mention its institution, but he records a wonderful discourse concerning the Bread of Life which is an indispensable commentary on the unnamed institution, and by filling in with great detail the circumstances of the last evening he furnished a framework for the ordinance which is among our most precious possessions. On the other hand, because the common tradition was very vague in its dates he gave precision to the event which they had recorded by fixing the time of its occurrence. This deserves a more detailed examination. It was very natural that the tradition, since it was known that the Lord came up to Jerusalem to eat the Passover, and that He actually had a Supper with His disciples, should suppose that the Supper was the Passover feast. The record in Matt. xxvi. 17, &c., seems to assume this as a matter of course. The disciples came and asked Him where He would eat the Passover; He gave them directions; "they made ready the Passover. Now when even was come, he was sitting at meat with the twelve disciples" and He instituted the Eucharistic feast. The narrative in Mark xiv. 12, &c., is to the same effect. The narrative in Luke xxii. is more explicit still. The author had evidently inferred from his authorities that the Last Supper was actually the Passover feast, and accordingly we read "with desire I have desired to eat this passover with you before I suffer" (ver. 15). No reader of these narratives would for a moment question that Jesus actually ate the Passover. But it seems this was an error. He sent His disciples to make ready the Passover, and the night before He had Supper with them in the prepared room; and no doubt He said that He had desired to eat the Passover with them; but He did not eat it with them, for He Himself was, that year, to be the Passover Lamb, and on the afternoon of the very evening on which all Judaism would keep the feast, somewhere about the time "between the evenings" when the lambs were killed, He, the

Lamb of God, was to die upon the cross. All this is made very plain in the narrative of our fourth Gospel. In chapter xviii. 28 we read how in the morning after the Last Supper the Jews "led Jesus from Caiaphas into the Prætorium, and it was early; and they themselves entered not into the Prætorium that they might not be defiled, but might eat the Passover," which shows that the Passover was yet to be eaten.

As the common tradition was not clear about the day, so it was not quite sure of the time of the Crucifixion. In Matt. xxvii. 45 we read that the darkness which covered the land came from the *sixth* to the *ninth* hour. And so says Mark xv. 33; and this latter Gospel also says that the crucifixion occurred at the *third* hour. By this we should suppose that the cross was reared at nine o'clock in the morning, and the darkness covered the land from midday to three o'clock. The fourth Gospel seems to purposely correct this impression when it tells us (xix. 14) that at the *sixth* hour the inquiry was still proceeding before Pilate, and shortly after "he delivered him unto them to be crucified." It is by this correction of the hour of the day that the beautiful fact is established to which reference was just made, the fact that the Lord died in the evening when the lamb for the Passover was being slain throughout the Jewish world.

It may be interesting while we are on this subject to give another illustration or two of this modifying or correcting work which is part of the function of our fourth Gospel. We may take an instance which brings out with some clearness the difference between the Triple Narrative compiled, if we may say so, from notes, and the Single Narrative coming from an original source. In Matt. iv. 12 and in Mark i. 14 the Temptation, just after Christ's Baptism, is immediately followed by the statement, "When he heard that John was delivered up, he withdrew into Galilee, and leaving Nazareth he came and dwelt in Capernaum." But this summary narrative had excluded one of the most interesting features of the early ministry of Jesus. Accordingly the fourth Gospel enlarges the story and emphasizes the marks of time. After the Baptism, according to this authority, Jesus "went down to Capernaum, he, and his mother, and his brethren, and his disciples, and there they abode not many days" (ii. 12). Then He went up to the Passover at Jerusalem, where He had the interview with Nicodemus. After that He went into the country districts of Judæa, "and John was baptizing in Ænon," and then the writer adds, as if his eye were on the condensed and misleading narrative of the common tradition, "for John was not yet cast into prison." The two great Teachers, the Forerunner and the greater than-he, were actually baptizing side by side (iii. 22–30), and it was because Jesus saw His reputation overshadowing John's that He voluntarily withdrew into Galilee, passing through Samaria.

So that while there were two journeys to Galilee before John was imprisoned, and that early period of the life was full of unique and wonderful interest, all had been compressed and crushed into the brief statement of Matt. iv. 12; Mark i. 14. In this case we seem to see the Evangelist deliberately loosening and breaking up the current history in order that he might insert into the cramped and lifeless framework some of the most valuable episodes of the Lord's life. If our fourth Evangelist had treated the Triple Narrative in the way that many of us had treated it, regarding it as a sin against the Holy Spirit to suggest that there was any incompleteness or any misleading abbreviations in it, we should have lost the wonderful accounts of the conversations with Nicodemus and with the woman at the well.

To take one more instance of a slightly different kind. The first Gospel in the tenth chapter gives a series of wonderful sayings which the Lord addressed to His disciples immediately after the completion of the number of the Twelve. In the course of these sayings, this occurs (ver. 17), "Beware of men, for they will deliver you up to the councils, and in their synagogues they will scourge you," and it goes on to describe very graphically the persecution to which the disciples will be subjected. Certainly there seems a little hardness in this: the ignorant men taken from the fishing-boat and the receipt of custom are, according to this, met from the first with a terrible forecast of all the sufferings they were likely to encounter. Very different is the impression given in the fourth Gospel of the first calling of the disciples. In an atmosphere of almost mystical tenderness, which is like a canvas of Perugino's, the first followers are drawn to the Lamb of God which taketh away the sins of the world. All was attraction, and beauty, and love (John i. 35–51). And it was not until months of intercourse had moulded and tempered the spirits of the men, that at last, when He was about to leave them and to send the Comforter, He drew aside the veil which hid the future, and let them know that tribulation awaited them (ch. xvi. 2), graciously adding, "And these things I said not unto you from the beginning, because I was with you." "In the world ye have tribulation: but be of good cheer; I have overcome the world." It was very natural that those earlier narratives, written perhaps when the first persecutions of the Church at Jerusalem or at Rome were fresh in every one's mind, should throw back the sad warnings which the Lord gave to His disciples to the very first day of their calling. But how beautiful is the correction which the clearer and more chronological narrative makes! It shows us a consideration on the part of the Lord which is true to all we know of Him. He was full of grace and truth.

It is very instructive to examine such an event as the anointing of the feet, recorded in Matt. xxvi. (Mark xiv. 3), and to see how the fourth

Evangelist seems to give life and animation to it by knowing that it was Mary who sat at Jesus' feet that anointed them. It is equally instructive to examine such narratives as the healing of the centurion's son (servant), or the miraculous feeding of the multitude, first in the three Gospels and then in the fourth. The harmonists usually maintain that the differences in the two versions point to duplicate events; but we have seen enough of the way in which the fourth Gospel deals with the others to accept the much simpler explanation. And when once this way of comparing the two becomes recognized, it will not be thought necessary, because the fourth Gospel corrects the mistake in the time of the cleansing of the Temple by placing it at the beginning of the Lord's ministry, to which it must surely belong, to maintain that there were *two* cleansings, one at the beginning and another at the end—an explanation which an *à priori* theory of Inspiration may demand, but none the less an explanation which must always appear very strained; for if the Inspired Biography meant to record a double cleansing, it would almost inevitably in narrating the second have alluded to the first. As it is, the Triple Narrative (Matt. xxi. 12; Mark xi. 15; Luke xix. 45) records the event at the end, without any sign that it had occurred at the beginning of the ministry; and we can only suppose that the notable fact had got misplaced in the Common Tradition from the circumstance that the Common Tradition did not record the early labours in Jerusalem, but seemed to suppose that the Lord only went up to Jerusalem towards the end of the third year's ministry.

Now in all that has been said about the fourth Gospel, we have avoided speaking of John as the author, for the very simple reason that the Gospel itself avoids speaking of John as the author, and thereby seems to imply that the validity of the narrative is not to be made dependent on the authorship. Tradition has never hinted at any other authorship, it is true; the signs that the disciple who testified these things was one of the immediate followers and friends of Jesus are very remarkable and numerous, it is true; the way in which the disciple whom Jesus loved is referred to without a name, while other disciples are named constantly, suggests that the anonymous disciple is the writer, it is true; but for all this we must be making a great mistake in choosing the Johannine authorship as our battle-ground in the controversy about this Gospel, if the Gospel itself so scrupulously abstains from claiming that ground. Just as we have seen in the three other Gospels, so we see here, the Inspired Biography does not choose to rest its authority upon any expressed authorship. But in this fourth Gospel there is a distinction. The author does in more than one place speak as an eye-witness, and assert his right to speak on that ground; and in a curious note added to the book (ch. xxi. 24) some unknown persons subscribe their testimonial to his veracity and authenticity. "We know," they say, "that his witness is true." We are thus, in common honesty, bound to regard this as the writing of an eye-witness, unless the contrary can be proved. But the contrary cannot be proved. Arguments *à priori* are worth nothing at all in such a case. We may with a kind of quiet confidence watch the battle of criticism raging around this point.

We can now, then, proceed in a sentence or two to bring together and compare the Triple and the Single Narratives. We find the two are not in complete accord; but the narrative of the eye-witness must clearly be taken as the standard by which the narrative which advances no such claim is to be tried. Here we seem to touch a guiding clue in the reading of the Inspired Biography. We find, further, that the three narratives, where they leave the common thread, show considerable and even irreconcilable divergences; and they seem therefore in an emphatic way to warn us against depending upon isolated verbal clauses in drawing our conclusions from them. We find, in fact, that instead of a biography in the modern sense, we have the materials for a biography put into our hand. That the materials are sufficient, all of us who have patiently and reverently studied them allow. By means of them we are enabled to bring before our eyes the historic Jesus, to observe His manner, to comprehend His teaching.

When, further, we come to combine the Single Narrative with the Triple Narrative, we obtain an insight into the thought and the consciousness of the historic Jesus. His outlines are not doubtful; His sayings and teachings are quickly recognizable, for they are spirit and they are life. That He is "miraculous," in the common acceptation of that term, is put beyond question. To attempt to interpret him as an ordinary man, or even as an extraordinary man, is to falsify the whole record, and so to reduce Him at once to an unknowable quantity. We are on the horns of a dilemma from which there is no escape: either this record is historical, or it is not. If it is, Jesus is the unique Son of God manifest in the flesh; if it is not, we have no knowledge of Jesus, we can say nothing about Him. To say that He is a man means nothing; it will go for no more than if we say that Heracles, or any other shadowy figure of an exploded mythology, is a man.

The materials are sufficient, patiently and earnestly studied, to reveal Jesus to us, and that is all we want. With Him we have everything. With Jesus revealed, we then have to realize that He is more than any detail about Him; acts in the record attributed to Him are sure and authentic in proportion as they are really in keeping with Him; sayings occurring in His lips come with authority in proportion as we recognize that it is from His lips that they come.

And thus, if we were to be asked what do we

mean by the inspiration of the four Gospels, we should be inclined to answer: "We mean that these historic writings have preserved for us in a sufficient and recognizable way the Life of the Lord from Heaven, so that by studying them we see and hear Him; and seeing that He is the very Word of God, the records which tell us what He was and what He said are *inspired*, not in a vague and indefinite sense, but in the literal sense that the Spirit of God Himself is speaking through them, albeit the actual writing was done by human hands and the literary composition was the work of human brains."

In leaving this part of the subject, we may perhaps observe how much we should have preferred a Life of Christ in the Inspired Book free from all difficulties; a life which would have made all the attempts that are constantly being made to write such a life unnecessary. But even in this it does not seem difficult to surmise a beautiful purpose of our Father in Heaven. The very difficulties of the Gospel narrative are a remarkable incentive to studying it. During all the untroubled ages of dreamy dogmatism the narrative was never scanned, and weighed, and searched as it has been since Paulus began to rationalize it, and Strauss to treat it as a myth, and Baur to explain it on a tendency-theory. Possibly even the hints thrown out in the present chapter, the facts alluded to which are not generally noticed, may rouse the reader to a more diligent search of the unparalleled Biography.

And the more it is searched, the more wonderful it appears. There may be a point in our inquiry at which an inaccurate genealogy, or a misplaced incident, or an ill-recorded speech, or an interpolated passage, seems to shake the whole fabric and imperil faith in the Gospel ; but as the great Form becomes clearer, as the impression of the whole is allowed quietly to settle down upon the spirit, one feels increasingly that here we have a possession of which no rationalism can rob us, and which criticism will only define and make more precious. For candid admission of fact and resolute laying aside of prejudice, undoubtedly we have our reward.

CHAPTER IV.

ON THE NEW TESTAMENT IN GENERAL.

IN the last two chapters we have taken examples of the way in which the New Testament literature must be searched before we can give body and colour to our idea of Inspiration. Starting with the assurance that the collection of writings as a whole is what we call 'inspired,' we took two parts of it and examined the phenomena they presented as a step towards defining what must be meant by 'inspired.' We took an unquestioned Epistle of Paul's, and we took the fourfold work which records the life of Jesus, and we ran through some of the points which are most striking in the composition and character of the books.

Here there comes a hiatus in our work. We ought to subject each book of the New Testament in turn to a similar investigation; we ought to consider its authorship, the circumstances of its composition, and the features which it presents, then we ought to bring together and classify our results, and to take care that all the facts established in the inquiry should find place in our conception of Inspiration. This, however, would be a very long inquiry, and would turn this little volume into an elaborate treatise. As we must relinquish the inviting task, it is necessary to point out where the hiatus exists, and to remind ourselves that we have done nothing more than suggest the lines on which the inquiry would have to move if the hiatus were to be filled. But while we are forced to leave the work in this incomplete state—a mere choir or transept of a church as the promise of a church which is to be—it may be possible in this brief chapter to sketch the outlines of the part that is to be left untouched; or at any rate we may venture on certain conjectures as to what the results would lead us to. In doing this we must be very careful to distinguish between what we are now about and what we have been about before. The two previous chapters have been a rigorous study of facts in which hypothesis has only played a supplementary part; the present chapter is only tentative and conjectural; its conclusions do not lay claim to be anything more than suggestions, and indeed it would be better to leave it unread than to be in any way bound to it: better not to accept the writer's hints at all, than to allow them to settle down into the mind as a dogma without further inquiry and correction. No, in this chapter there is nothing, and can be nothing, dogmatic. Perhaps the time has hardly yet come when even Biblical scholars could formulate a complete theory. We may rear a temporary and provisional building, but it is mischievous if it makes us forget that the real building is still to be reared. From what we have already seen, we shall be prepared for the conclusion that the New Testament writings as a whole bear what may be called an occasional character; that is to say, so far from the New Testament being a set homogeneous composition, even its several parts can hardly be said to answer to that description. No part of the collection is more like a set treatise than the great Epistle to the Romans; but it is remarkable that even this is so mingled with the occasional element that it almost seems as if we had got at the end of it a series of postscripts. There are, if we may say so, three endings—one at chapter xv. 33, another at xvi. 20, a third at xvi. 27. The conclusion is almost irresistible that this remarkable letter had been copied out and sent to many churches, and then, when the collection of the Pauline Epistles was to be made, three copies appeared, each with a different ending adapted to the church to which it was directed; and the compiler or editor, not liking to lose a word of the apostle's, tacked together the three endings when the Epistle was published. Thus, from all we know of the persons named, we should say that the termination xvi. 1–20 was addressed not to the Roman but to the Ephesian Christians. In any case, this addition of postscript to postscript, this dropping fire of last words, reminds us how little the writer thought of even this set treatise being a permanent literary work.

But while this limitation has to be recognized in the claim of the Romans to being a set composition, we must recognize that the other writings of the New Testament are still further removed from that character. No Gospel gives a settled and connected life of Jesus. Even the fourth, which has more the air of a treatise, is, as we have seen, almost of the nature of a supplement, and it has tacked on to it an addition which is avowedly an afterthought. The Acts of the Apostles is so far from being what we should call a piece of philosophical history, that we are surprised to find in the midst of it the writer appearing as one of the actors in the story, and again disappearing and reappearing without any direct statement who he is. And not to dwell on the divergences of the narrative from other sources in the New Testament, *e.g.*, the account of the Ascension, the account of the Council at Jerusalem, the account of St. Paul's visit to Jerusalem, the book itself closes abruptly, as if the author had been suddenly stricken down or silenced ; and all we can say about it is that this could never have been the intended termination of such a narrative. As to the Epistles,—leaving out of account the one to the Romans,—the two to the Corinthians, the one to the Galatians, the one to the Philippians, and the two to the Thessalonians are quite of the nature of a private correspondence. They are personal and particular ; broad and general principles are introduced into them by way of episode ; the main subject is the condition of the particular church addressed. The same may be said, in a less degree, of the Epistles to the Ephesians and the Colossians. In the Epistle to the Hebrews we seem to find a writing which bears more the nature of a treatise; in fact it scarcely betrays any signs of being an Epistle in our understanding of the word. But it is remarkable that this beautiful and interesting tract is mainly occupied with what we may call a secondary issue; it is an apologetic writing which aims at conciliating the Jews whom Paul had exasperated; it shows how Christianity was implicit in Judaism. The remaining letters of the collection have no appearance of doctrinal treatises; though with the exception of ii. and iii. John, Philemon and the three Pastoral Letters, they are addressed to the Christian community at large, and not to any particular church, the Epistles of James, Peter, i. John, and Jude, are as far removed from being theological works in our sense of the word, as tracts issued in our own day for general distribution. All we can say is that in them we are presented with three, if not four, curiously different standpoints from which Christian truth and Christian life may be surveyed. The Apocalypse stands apart in the New Testament, though by no means alone in the early Christian literature. On one interpretation of it, the interpretation which sees in it a vivid picture of the conflict between the Church and the great Roman World Power, it too is an occasional writing, though it is true that many Bible students find in it a prophecy not of "the things which must shortly come to pass," as the book says itself (i. 1, cf. xxii. 10-12, 20), but of the events which have been happening ever since and which are yet to happen. Leaving aside the Apocalypse, as a writing about the interpretation of which there is no unanimity among students, but rather the very broadest divergency, we may, in this brief survey, recognize the singularly occasional character of our New Testament literature. There is, if we may say so reverently, a certain haphazard appearance, the appearance of a collection of remnants, remnants gathered together at a time when it was felt that if they were not then gathered they would disappear; gathered therefore with a certain fostering care which did not inquire closely whether the several pieces conformed to a certain preconception of them, but was eager to secure all that *bore a certain stamp*, and which brought them into one volume on the ground of their bearing that stamp. That stamp, no doubt, is what we recognize as Inspiration, but the character and the method of the collection give rise to the difficulty of determining exactly what that inspiration is.

It is from this haphazard character of the writings that the task of constructing a theological system, a formulated set of doctrines, out of the New Testament is rendered next to impossible. It is a matter for mirth to the unbeliever to point to Christian thinkers drawing their different and contradictory theologies from the same very limited set of sacred writings.

> "Hic liber est in quo quærit sua dogmata quisque
> Invenit et pariter dogmata quisque sua."[1]

Calvin was quite sure it taught a salvation wrought out only for the elect, and Arminius was equally sure its salvation was for all; Calvinists and Arminians accordingly hated one another, and thereby violated its one quite indubitable commandment that we are to love one another. Episcopalianism declares it teaches Apostolic Succession; Congregationalism believes it quite denies any order of Bishops or Priests in the Christian Communities: and thereby they hold aloof from one another, and bring shame upon their Lord who declared they all should be one. Universalists maintain that it teaches the restoration of all human souls; another party says it teaches the eternal death of those who are not in Christ; another that it teaches their eternal torment. Now considering the whole of the Volume from which the combatants draw their weapons for these secular disputes is barely two hundred octavo pages, and is for the most part, when properly translated, as plain and simple writing as one would wish to read, it is not perhaps a very bold conclusion to arrive at, that the Volume never meant to give a clear utterance on these questions; that in fact its nature and its origin as a collection of diverse writings actually prevented it from ever serving these ends of controversy. We may

[1] "This is the book where each his dogmas seeks:
Each finds the book his own pet dogma speaks."

say with confidence that the careful study of the New Testament on the lines laid down in the two preceding chapters will necessarily open our eyes to a very remarkable discovery, viz., that these bitter and saddening contentions never could have arisen if the first step had been to ask what the New Testament *actually is*. The whole of this polemical theology which has disgraced the Church of Christ and turned our attention aside from practical duty, so that the world remains unconverted, and educated Europe is smiling contemptuously upon us, may be traced to that radically false assumption, an assumption made from the beginning without any attempt at proof, that by an Inspired New Testament must be meant a homogeneous treatise on theology which would authoritatively give us a Doctrine and a Church Government divinely ordained and unquestionable, to which all must submit as to the Word of God.

Our searchings have shown us, on the other hand—and if they were carried further they would show us still more clearly—that the writers of the New Testament were by no means equipped to give us a scheme of authoritative dogma. Each of them is limited by his own limitations and the limitations of his circumstances : we may be sure they would have been horrified if they could have foreseen how casual words of theirs were to be used as weapons or as party cries to harass and divide the flock of their Lord. What are we to say of religious teachers who claim a Divine authority, first for every verse of the Old Testament, and then for every verse of the New Testament, and yet have never noticed that the New Testament writers only very occasionally quote the Old Testament writings correctly? We can only say that our teachers in their blindness have dishonoured the Book which they thought they were defending. St. Paul, for instance, seldom quotes from the Hebrew Bible at all, but almost always from the Septuagint, that unintelligent and in places unintelligible Greek version of the Bible which was current in the Hellenistic world, the version which in the darker days of Inspirational Dogma was actually declared to be itself inspired.[1] And if the quotation of a New Testament writer is to be taken as a guarantee for the writing quoted, then we should have to say that Jude (verses 9 and 14) puts his seal to those apocryphal writings, the Book of Enoch and the Assumption of Moses, which are referred to in his Epistle. Nor is it only in quotation that the New Testament writers present a caution to dogmatic theologians; in the interpretation of Old Testament passages, and notably of prophecies, they followed the method which was current in their own day, a method which reverent students of the Bible will often try to avoid as peculiarly dangerous. The allegorizing which St. Paul allows himself in the

[1] Cf. Eph. v. 14, which seems to be an apocryphal quotation due to a *lapsus memoriæ*.

Epistle to the Galatians, and the use of merely verbal quotations wrenched from their context which Matthew, for example, sometimes makes (cf. Matt. i. 23 with Isa. vii. 14, or still more surprising, Matt. ii. 15 with Hosea xi. 1), cannot be regarded as authoritative models for our own treatment of the Old Testament writings. That an *à priori* theory of inspiration required men to treat these and similar passages as the interpretation which the Holy Ghost gave of His own writings, will be one day almost as incredible as it already is that the opponents of Copernicus gravely and honestly quoted Scripture in disproof of the earth's rotation round the sun.

In a word, the searching of the New Testament on the lines that have been suggested must lead us to regard with suspicion the whole method of constructing systems of Theology, or Ecclesiasticism, or Eschatology, out of the texts of the Sacred Writings, as a method which is from the first discouraged and rendered practically impossible by the nature of the writings themselves. The truth is the New Testament contains within itself dynamic forces which always shatter any neatly constructed system compiled from it. Luther's re-discovery of St. Paul split the Catholic Church and produced the Reformation. The fresh and eager study of the Gospels has in our day shattered the dogmatic system of the Reformers. The Eternal Punishment dogma is broken upon the conceptions of the Divine Nature which the unprejudiced reading of the New Testament itself creates. The hierarchical Church which has quoted an isolated text from St. Matthew (xvi. 18) as its foundation, and the Pastoral Epistles as its bulwarks, is convulsed with threatenings of doom when the careful study of the four Gospels compels us to place the isolated text in its due perspective, and when the study and comparison of the Letters of St. Paul and the records of his life reveal that these Pastoral Letters, even if they meant what Catholicism reads into them, are precisely the most uncertain and least authoritative parts of the Pauline collection. The study of the New Testament is what always brings new vigour into flagging Christendom, and though it usually produces as a first result a rapid undermining of the systems which have been constructed, it never fails to quicken the spirit and to enlarge the borders of the Christian Community.

And this leads us to characterize the New Testament as a whole, that book which we have seen reason to believe is so widely different from what we should expect it to be, and from what many of us, following an *à priori* theory instead of the facts, have actually convinced ourselves that it is.

The New Testament is, as we have said, a collection of writings gathered together (presumably towards the end of the second century) on the ground that they bore *a certain stamp*. What was this stamp? What was the occasion of the collection? These questions we will try to answer, taking the last first. From the Apostolic teaching such as that contained in ii. Thess. ii. 1–12, and implied in the reported discourses of Jesus, and the closing chapter of the Apocalypse, the first generation of Christians expected an immediate Parousia, or appearance and presence of the Risen Christ. Very few, possibly none, saw that the expectation was fulfilled in the destruction of Jerusalem in the year 70 A.D., though an expressly recorded saying of Jesus (Matt. xxiv. 34) might have led them to that conclusion. The expectation of the second coming lingered and gave to the Christian churches a feeling that the time was short, and no provision for a distant future need be made. But when the circle of the eye-witnesses of the Life of Jesus and of the apostolic preachers, including St. Paul, had actually died out, and still the end had not come, it became clear that at any rate their own generation must be supplied with the authentic narratives and teachings of the immediate witnesses. This seems to have been the motive in the careful guarding, and ultimately in the collection into one volume, of apostolic writings. A gospel narrative which passed as a composition of an apostle, like John or Matthew, or of an apostle's secretary or companion, like Mark and Luke, was treasured as a priceless record for the time when no living voice could tell what the disciples saw and heard. Letters written by apostles, or under the supervision of apostles, were treasured for the same reason. The collection of writings therefore was preserved as the apostolic witness to Christ. No one of these writings was written to form a part of the collection ; and this accounts for their occasional character. But every scrap of narrative, or exhortation, or correction, or personal episode, which came from the apostles and prophets who were the foundation of that building of which Jesus Christ was the chief corner-stone, was reverently treasured up. In the first instance there was no idea of putting the collection on a level with the Inspired Hebrew Scriptures ; that was a development which we can even now trace with some accuracy. But the apostolic writings were the witness to Christ, they were the mirrors set at different angles, in which the Divine Person was reflected. The discrepancies of the fragmentary narratives, or the imperfections of apostolic reasonings, were held of secondary importance, mere inequalities or cracks in the mirrors, which did not materially distort or hide the Person ; and besides, if the distortion had been more serious than it was, this was all that was to be had ; it must be the Christ reflected in these records of His immediate followers, or the Christ of a mere tradition ; and tradition is always liable to change, and is always threatened with oblivion.

When we come to consider the matter in this way, the incalculable importance of the New Testament writings emerges into view, while at the same time the many difficulties connected with it receive some sort of an explanation. Here in a word is the historic witness to a Person, to the Person from whom issue the influences which recreated the world, which made a religion, which live and breathe upon us still, and which never showed such incalculable powers as just now when science *seems* to have made faith in the supernatural difficult, and criticism *seems* to have taken from us our Inspired Volume.

Perhaps the second question, What is the stamp upon these writings which determined their selection? hardly seems to require a separate answer after what has just been said. But the answer is not to be evaded; it is rendered necessary by certain rather notable facts. There were writings which passed as emanating from the apostolic circle, which yet have not maintained their place in what we call the Canon. To mention only two, we still possess a letter of Clement of Rome, and a letter of Barnabas. Why should not these writings which were held to come from the immediate companions of St. Paul have found a place in the apostolic records? Or to look in another direction, we have traces of several other Gospels, such, for instance, as the Gospel of the Hebrews or the Gospel of Nicodemus, which in the first ages were hardly distinguished from the Four as authoritative narratives. Why were these left out of the account, while the Four were retained? Now a satisfactory answer cannot be given to these very reasonable inquiries on merely critical grounds. It is clearly not enough to say that the Epistle to the Hebrews was admitted because, though the work of Apollos or Barnabas, it was attributed to St. Paul, while the Epistle of Barnabas was excluded because it was recognized as coming from his pen. There would always remain the further question, Why should St. Paul be admitted and not St. Barnabas, for the first was actually introduced to the Church by the last, and neither was an actual witness of the Lord's life as the Twelve were? It is not enough to say that our second and third Gospels were admitted because their authors were held to have been companions of Peter and Paul; for on that showing the Gospel of Nicodemus had a higher claim, since the reputed author was in close connection with Jesus Himself.

In a word, the answer which criticism gives to our questions about the choice of books to form the Canon is itself always open to criticism. Every answer attempted raises a further question. Apostolic authorship may account for the presence of ii. and iii. John, ii. Peter, Jude, or even James in the Canon; but it does not account for the presence of the much more important letters of Paul. It may account for the first and fourth Gospels, but it does not account for the second and third. The answer which we should be inclined to give is one which at first appears vague and unsatisfactory, but grows clearer the more we examine it.

There is a certain stamp upon the writings which were selected to permanently represent the apostolic record, a certain intrinsic character, a note by which their relation to one another and their separation from the other contemporary writings may be distinguished. The note of the New Testament writings is immediately perceptible when we turn to even the best of what are called the Apostolic Fathers. It is our own judgment no less than that of those who first collected the New Testament scriptures, that the Epistles of Clement and Barnabas belong to a different order, have altogether a different note. To further specify the note of the New Testament is exceedingly difficult. It baffles analysis very much as the note of true poetry baffles analysis. It is a certain insight, a certain essential veracity, a certain revealing quality. It is not, we have seen, an immunity from all human imperfections, but it is a partaking of certain Divine perfections. It is a speaking about Christ which becomes in the reading Christ speaking about Himself. It is a voice rather than a reasoning; it is recognized rather by an intuition than by a judgment. Yet few careful students of the New Testament have failed to recognize it, and the comparison between the New Testament on the one hand, and the Apocryphal Gospels and sub-apostolic literature on the other, seems to place it, however undefinable it may be, beyond possibility of question. We cannot say that this note of the New Testament is equally perceptible in all the writings. To take an instance which readily occurs, the two Epistles ii. Peter and Jude in a very slight degree betray this note; we may surmise, therefore, that they owe their present position rather to their apostolic names than to their apostolic spirit. But the recognition of some New Testament writings as being without the note, or as rendering it but faintly, only brings into stronger relief the note which is perceptible in the whole.

We cannot say, perhaps, that if we had before us to-day all the writings which were current when the New Testament was formed we should choose exactly what were then chosen, and exclude exactly what were then excluded; but we can safely say that following the principles which must have led to the formation of this Volume, and, above all, observing the stamp which is impressed upon the several compositions, we should now, apart from all prejudice, make a collection which would be practically identical with the New Testament as it stands.

In this chapter, which covers the hiatus in our work, we have avowedly been treading on conjectural grounds; but enough has been said to show that the rigorous application of an Inductive Method to the phenomena of the New Testament, in order to find what is to be understood by its inspiration, is not likely to lessen our wonder at the Sacred Volume, but may not improbably save us from certain illicit uses to which we have sometimes put it.

CHAPTER V.

OF THE OLD TESTAMENT: THE PROPHET IN THE INSPIRED BOOK.

WHEN we turn from the Christian literature collected in the New Testament to the literature in the Old Testament, we turn from a comparatively simple and terminable task to one that is exceedingly complex and well-nigh interminable. The variety of literary form; the uncertain but very considerable period of time over which the writings are spread; the obscurity which shrouds the origin, authorship, and date of a large number of the books; and, in fact, many other difficulties which hardly allow themselves to be classified, may well make us halt, and wonder whether, within the scope of this little volume, we can hope to touch the subject to any useful purpose. We all—that is to say all who profess and call themselves Christians—attach a vague but unquestioned authority to the whole volume of Old Testament writings: as we put it in brief—the Volume is inspired. But when we come, upon the principles which we are at present following, to ask what features are to be included in this conception, or, indeed, what characteristics go to make the conception, we are quite baffled by the number and the intricacy of the problems which immediately present themselves. We believe that our Lord recognized the authority of these writings. We find in the Apostolic literature two comparatively clear statements, and many side hints, that the first believers recognized their authority, and actually applied to them an epithet which is never applied to any writings in the New Testament itself, an epithet which we render "inspired of God." The idea of inspiration therefore attaches by prescription even more strongly to the Old Testament than to the New. But this very confidence in speaking of it as inspired makes it all the more imperative to examine closely what the inspiration must be held to convey and what it must not. There is no rough and ready method. What is demanded of us is the calm, patient, and earnest consideration of each book by itself. We ought to get all the light we can upon its authorship, its composition, its date, its immediate purpose; we ought to note all the literary phenomena that it presents; and only when all these facts have been considered and classified, and allowed to subside into their due and proportionate places, shall we be able to give a full and right content to the idea of Inspiration applied to the Old Testament. Considering the great difficulty of this task, we are not to wonder that men have thought to simplify it by taking a short cut : they have, for instance, borrowed ideas of inspiration from heathenism, from the ecstatic phrensy of the Delphic priestess, from the popular conception of inspired Vedas, or even from the notion of inspiration which Mahomet ingeniously created in composing the Koran. "This is what *we* mean by inspiration," have said these teachers who mean to go by the short cut. "Our Old Testament is inspired; therefore"—and it is plain that the conclusion is very logically drawn from the premisses—"*therefore* the Old Testament is inspired in this way." Accordingly we have sometimes been led to conceive of Moses seated with parchment and pen before him, writing the Pentateuch as a Spirit dictated it to him, in a complete disregard of any documents, or traditions, or observations which an ordinary writer would have employed. In the same way we have been led to suppose that the historical books flowed from a Divinely-directed pen which had to take no counsel with archives or dates, because, apart from the will of the writer, all facts and all chronologies would be guaranteed by the Spirit of God. We have been given to understand that Job wrote down a verbal record of his dialogue with his friends, the Holy Spirit recalling every word just as it had been uttered : or more strangely still, it has been made almost an article of faith to picture King David writing down the Psalter, very much as the Sybil of Cumæ uttered her inspired oracles. And so on with prophets, and poets, and preachers. But indeed it would take us much too far afield to even glance at the innumerable crude conceptions that we have acquired simply from the habit—so facile, so delusive—of starting with an idea of what the Inspired Book ought to be, instead of patiently and laboriously discovering what the Inspired Book is.

Perhaps a little roughness of dogmatism may be pardoned in this place, considering the lethargic condition of thought upon the subject. Perhaps we may say—and challenge any confutation of the principle—that *every fact which the most fearless criticism, historical, scientific, or literary, is able to establish concerning our Old Testament, is to be humbly accepted, and our idea of inspiration is to be shaped, or re-shaped, in order to include it.* " Is able to establish," be it observed, not merely able to suggest. But such facts can only be arrived at by the free use of hypotheses, many of which must be removed as the work proceeds, just as scaffolding is removed when it has served its purpose. The fearless criticism which has for long been playing upon the Scriptures is not to be resented. Its conclusions are to be tested, and held in suspense until they are established. But if they are established, they will only be an enrichment of our knowledge; they cannot in any way rob us of our Book. The Book was there to start with; it will be there when criticism has done. Criticism will only have shown us more clearly what is in the Book.

But at present we are concerned with the question, How are we to set about an investigation of these diversified writings ; where should we begin, and how should we proceed ? It might at first sight appear that our best way would be to begin with the Book of Genesis and go straight on, working through the Bible as we have it in one volume. But for our purpose this would be a very confusing method of procedure. The Pentateuch, as it lies before us, is the Law Book of Judaism ; that is, the Law Book of the Second Temple, of the restored exiles, of the post-prophetic Church, of the Jewish polity of our Lord's day. It is placed first in the Jewish Bible because its authority was held superior to that of all other writings ; the Volume of the Prophets, and the volume of the other books—the Hagiographa, as they were called—occupying a secondary position. This Sacred Law, guarded by Judaism with a scrupulous care, was never made the subject of critical inquiries. No one asked who wrote it. It was assumed that the earthly founder of the nation of Israel, Moses, had written it. Accordingly no one ever asked when it was written. The unquestioning Jewish tradition that Moses wrote it was naturally accepted in perfect good faith until it occurred to some minds to inquire on what the tradition rested At once it appeared that no answer could be given to the inquiry, for the Pentateuch itself gave no answer. Nowhere does the author declare himself ; everywhere appear indications which make the Mosaic authorship questionable. The question is now under earnest discussion; the dogmatic slumber in which Jewish tradition was allowed to pass as Divine authority has been disturbed; but no generally accepted answer has yet been given. It would therefore be needlessly perplexing to start in our inquiry with a book which presents such special difficulties. The book relates to the earliest times, it is true; but if we were reviewing Roman literature, for instance, and trying to understand it in its continuity, we should not begin with Livy because his narrative opens with the foundation of Rome; we should begin with the earliest authors whose date could be with some certainty fixed. It is this consideration—in the main the same consideration which led us to start in the New Testament with St. Paul rather than with the Gospels—it is this consideration which makes the writings of the Prophets much the most convenient starting-point for our inquiry. In the prophets we have men speaking about the things which were before their own eyes, placing their readers in the midst of circumstances which were the forming influences of their own lives and works. In many cases the dates are fixed with certainty; in most cases the prophet himself affords us a clear view of his own personality.

In the Prophetic writings, therefore, we have a peculiarly firm ground to stand upon; we have a historic situation; we are enabled to get into the life of the times; and from that standpoint we are better prepared for our labours in the more uncertain parts of the field. If we may use an illustration, it is like examining Wright's political songs in order to understand the day of the Plantagenets; only, of course, there is this consideration which makes the parallel very imperfect, no national songwriters ever wrote as the Prophets of Israel spoke: a very cursory reading of the books at once convinces every candid reader that here we have a style of writing, a style of speaking, a style of thinking, to which there is no adequate parallel elsewhere. And it is this, too, which further commends the Prophetic writings to us as a starting-point in our inquiry; with the authors of them we feel directly that we are dealing with inspired men. Not only, therefore, the historical solidity of the books, but even more their peculiar and impressive character, makes them specially suited for a clue to us in the search which must during this and the following chapters occupy our attention.

But if we are agreed to begin with the Prophets, it may at least be thought that we should take them in the order in which they occur in our Bible. This course, however, is not desirable. The order in which they occur in our Bible is singularly arbitrary. The four Great Prophets are put first, not because they are greater prophets, but because the books containing their prophecies are larger books. The twelve Minor Prophets are massed together, as it were, in one volume, not because their message was less important, but because their writings were briefer. By this unfortunate arrangement we are hindered from appreciating the relation in which the Prophets stand to one another. Where the same passages occur in more than one, we are apt to think that the author who comes later in our collection is quoting from the one who comes earlier there.

We ought to begin, therefore, by finding which are the earliest of the Prophetic writings in order of time. It seems probable that Obadiah and Joel should be put in this position; but still we cannot conveniently start with them, because neither of them tells us his date nor yet who he was. It is left, therefore, more as an inference than a demonstration that they belong to the time before the Assyrian invasion began to loom on the horizon of Israel's political world. It would seem, then, that the first convenient writing with which to begin in the Prophetic literature is the Book of Amos. Here we have something quite determinate. The author fixes his own date, and tells us a good deal about himself; and further, his writing is sufficiently brief and unified to enable us to deal with it in a very small compass.

Having seen reasons then for starting with the Prophetic literature in the Old Testament, we have been led to make a beginning in the Prophetic literature with the little Book of Amos.

If we can succeed in understanding the scope and the gist of this book, we must not think that we have got a key to the scope and gist of the other

Prophets, for they are varied, and each one has to be examined by himself; but we may reasonably hope that we shall get an idea of the method by which the scope and gist of the rest will have to be determined.

The first thing which strikes us about Amos is the origin of his prophetic office, if office it may be called. He was a working man. As he explained to the priest of the high place at Bethel, when the authorized functionary wished to silence the inconvenient seer, he was a herdman and dresser of sycamore trees, and was not connected by birth or training with prophets or prophetic schools. He derived his mission from the Lord; how, he does not explain; but the statement of fact is clear enough; "The Lord took me from following the flock, and the Lord said unto me, Go, prophesy unto my people Israel" (Amos vii. 15). It is noteworthy that the first quite determinate prophetic utterance which meets us in our examination of the Old Testament should be from an agricultural labourer. It would seem that the very essence of prophecy is the consciousness on the teacher's part of a message given to him by God Himself to deliver to the world.

Our prophet tells us with a similar explicitness the time in which his ministry was placed. The Kingdoms of Israel and Judah were still intact; the Kingdom of Judah very inferior and subordinate to the Kingdom of Israel, be it remembered. It was a time of great prosperity in the Northern

Kingdom; Jeroboam the Second had rolled back the tide of Syrian incursions, and had restored the border of Israel from the entering in of Hamath unto the sea of the Arabah. The fact was that the great Assyrian Monarchy was beginning to press upon Damascus, and as the Syrians withdrew to defend their own borders, they left Israel unmolested. This may be concluded from 2 Kings xiv 25, and from what the Assyrian monuments tell us of the movements of Salmaneser III. We must suppose ourselves at the beginning of the eighth century before Christ; to be definite, let us say about the year 780 B.C. The success of the arms of Israel against Syria was taken as a mark of the Divine favour; and as the people breathed afresh, quite regardless of the threat to themselves contained in the Assyrian victory over their troublesome neighbours, they fell into all the sins of luxury and licentiousness which follow too easily upon peace and prosperity. Social injustice and oppression, the invariable concomitants of luxury and licentiousness, made the life of the State rotten. The rich oppressed the poor, and even sold them into slavery; they ground them piteously into the dust, and exacted even "the dust on their heads;" they took the very garment in pledge; and with the money basely extorted they revelled in feasts in the high places of God (Amos ii. 6-8). The rich of the land were exceeding rich, and holding the judicial posts (v. 12) they turned them to account, shamelessly accepting bribes. They had mansions for summer and other mansions for winter; their rooms were furnished with ivory couches and silken cushions (iii. 12). And there the days passed in laziness and revelry, in light songs to the viol, in " devising instruments of music like David " (vi. 5). And all the shameful impurities which unequally distributed wealth brings in its train were exhibited among these great lords (ii. 7). We get a glimpse of the royal city, Samaria, seen from the circle of her hills; it is a city of palaces, and, like all cities of palaces which ever existed, there were "great tumults in it and oppressions in the midst thereof."

The peasant from Tekoah is sent to utter the indignation of the Lord against these wealthy, prosperous, selfish, luxurious, and cruel men. That is the situation. The prophetic word is the utterance of a lofty moral righteousness against the sins of the time, and the threat of doom which the sins are surely entailing. The word rolls like a thunder cloud round the nations which encompass Israel— Damascus to the north-east, Gaza to the south-west, Tyre to the north-west, Edom, Ammon, and Moab to the south-east, are successively denounced. The lightnings seem to fly across the holy land, and again across it. Shall the sacred land itself escape? No, in a yet more terrific peal Israel itself is assailed, as if it were one of the group of nations, not a favoured people at all, distinguished only by its excess of sinfulness (Amos ii. 6 *seq.*).[1]

---

[1] It may be noted that ii. 4, 5 seems to break the force of this storm-movement; possibly these two verses are an afterthought.

The threat upon the favoured people is distinct and unmistakable; they shall go away into captivity, ay, beyond Damascus (v. 27), they shall be among the first of all the group of nations to pass away to the conqueror's land (vi. 7).

We must notice, too, what the prophet had to say to the prevailing religious worship in the Northern Kingdom. There were evidently in his day several sanctuaries to which the people resorted. There was the king's sanctuary at Bethel (vii. 13). There was another at Gilgal (iv. 4, v. 5). There was one at Dan and another at Samaria (viii. 14). Finally, there is one mentioned at Beersheba (v. 5, viii., 14), which seems to have been connected with the story of Isaac (cf. vii. 9 with Gen. xxvi. 24). Now considering the attitude taken towards these High Places, or local sanctuaries, in the Book of Deuteronomy, where the whole of Israel is required to come up to one sanctuary and to use one altar, we should expect Amos, especially as he himself belonged to the Southern Kingdom of Judah, to inveigh against the very existence of the High Places. This, however, is not what he actually does. He seems to quite recognize the legitimacy of the sanctuaries, but his denunciations are directed against the practices which obtained in them; his scorn is roused by the very regularity and zeal with which the cultus is carried out. He ironically calls the people to bring the daily sacrifice, and to make their tithes payable every three days instead of every three years (iv. 4; see Deut. xxvi. 12), and to offer the leavened cakes with the free-will offerings: but all this regularity of worship will not avail in a land where injustice and cruelty run riot; it will not prevent the judgment which draws near; the sinful people, in spite of all their ceremonials, must prepare to meet their God.

In a word, the standpoint occupied by the prophet is distinctly ethical; it is the preaching of righteousness, the assertion of the futility which attaches to all religious worship and ceremonial unless the heart is right with God. The more the circumstances of the time, and the more the circumstances of the prophet are considered, the more strikingly is this feature of the situation brought out. It is the direct impulse from God in the man's heart; he cannot but speak; "The lion hath roared, who will not fear? The Lord God hath spoken, who can but prophesy?" (iii. 8). He might have chosen to live in peace among his own people in the little town among the hills of Judah, but a necessity was laid upon him; he was obliged to go and prophesy, to confront the bitter hostility of the nobles, the constituted religious leaders (vii. 10), and the people at large. The land was not able to bear his words; they were words which a land sunk in luxury and sensuality might well tremble at. They were no appeal to a traditional, still less to a written, law; there is no mention of the ordinances of Moses; no allusion to tabernacle or temple or ritual; the prophet speaks straight from the heart of the Holy Lord God all the eternal truth of the unwritten moral law. Herein lies his inspiration. Exigent indeed should we be if we demanded anything higher in inspiration. Even in our own day the message comes with freshness and force. After all the progress and spiritualization which are due to Christianity, we cannot say that Amos is at all superseded. He spoke to the prosperous, easy, sensual formalists of his own day; but his words still live and burn when addressed to the prosperous, easy, sensual formalists of all days, to men who have the form of godliness yet deny the power of it.

Familiarity can hardly be said to have removed the strangeness of the turn which the prophetic message takes, when it cries, "You only have I known of all the families of the earth; *therefore* will I visit upon you all your iniquities" (iii. 2). What an unexpected "therefore"! The election of Grace, then, is not an election to privilege so much as an election to chastisement and discipline. God has no favoured people in the common sense of the word; His favoured people are those whom He rebukes and chastens, in whom He can by no means bear iniquity. The announcement came like a thunder-clap to the people of Israel under Jeroboam II., whose idea of God was of a National Protector, a god of the land, who would fight the battles of the land, and if His sacrifices were duly offered would not be strict to mark iniquity The announcement comes as a thunder-clap to us still. The message has an eternal significance. It was a new idea of God to Israel; it is a new idea of God to many of us; a God who says, "Yea, though ye offer me your burnt offerings and meat offerings, I will not accept them; neither will I regard the peace offerings of your fat beasts. Take thou away from me the noise of thy songs; for I will not hear the noise of thy viols [the old joyous feast worship of Israel]. But let judgment roll down as waters, and righteousness as a mighty stream" (Amos v. 21–24). We might almost say that a voice which could say this again in our own day, which could declare the spirituality of God, and the stern moral demands of His religion, would be an inspired voice; how much more inspired must such a voice appear to us coming eight hundred years before Christ, speaking to a people whose ideas of God and goodness were at the best outward and imperfect, but, even such as they were, had become obscured by vice and self-indulgence?

The solitude of the herdsman prophet in protest against a corrupt kingdom will bear thinking of, and will seem more and more, the more it is thought of, to be a note of the highest inspiration. If we should go no farther, we should have attained at least one definite and even sufficient idea of what a prophetic inspiration means.

But we have not yet done with this wonderful little book. The dark and threatening cloud with which the prophecy opens " turns yet a silver lining on the night" before it closes. There is a brighter future in store, not, it is true, for the corrupt kingdom of Jeroboam, but for the smaller and more insignificant kingdom to which the prophet himself belongs. The "tabernacle of David" —or rather it is the "cottage of David"—the shrunken and feeble monarchy which had its centre at Jerusalem, was to be raised up, and the breaches thereof were to be closed. It did not come within the prophet's range of vision to know that a destruction, hardly less total than that which was prophesied for Jeroboam's people, must fall upon Judah also. Of a captivity for the holy city he clearly did not dream (ix. 15). But like a distant snow-peak, seen rosy red at sunset, over the dark circle of hills which shut in the valley, appears to him the brighter promise of David's House. How far off it was, of what nature it would be, how it would be realized, he did not know. But in that glowing picture of simple rural felicity—surpassing all that had been promised—the plowman following immediately on the reaper in the fertile fields, the vintage mingling with the seed time, and the fruitful hills clad in vine and olive melting with the richness of luscious fruitage, we seem to have a promise of more than is expressed. Some spirit seems to tell us that we are hearing of the far-off Kingdom of God, and by the "cottage of David" seems to be meant that house not made with hands which is now being raised by great David's Greater Son. This, however, was not, could not be intelligible to the contemporaries of the prophet, nor is there any indication that it was intelligible to Amos himself; so far as the form of the prediction goes, the hope is limited by the limitations of his own time; the most that is distinctly foreseen is the re-conquest of the remnant of Esau's people and of the petty nations that had been more or less influenced by Jehovah worship (ix. 12).

But it may be asked, Is this all we are to understand by the predictive powers of the prophet? Does not a prophet mean a foreteller? Does not the inspiration of the prophet consist in his miraculous foreknowledge of definite events which lie in the future? To these questions we cannot give any complete answer while we are concentrating our attention upon this particular prophet. In Amos, at any rate, there is no prediction of Christ or of Messianic times in so many words; there is no attempt to forecast the years, or to map out the future. But even in Amos there is that insight into the condition of the surrounding nations, as well as into the condition of his own nation, which impels him to "prophetic" utterances in the limited sense just mentioned. To these we may turn our attention for a moment, but we must be cautious in the insistence which we place upon the facts, because our records of the fulfilments of these predictions are not very full, nor can we be always sure how far they have been coloured by the predictions themselves. Historical books written after the time of Amos might be influenced by the predictions, and imagine a fulfilment in the events which they are recording, very much as modern interpreters of the Apocalypse find a variety of historical instances 'foretold,' as they curiously phrase it, in those mystic imageries.

The prophet—to come to examples—looking at the ruins of Gilead, which resulted from Hazael's successful invasion as recorded in 2 Kings x. 32, prophesies the destruction of the Syrian monarchy (i. 3–5) and the captivity of the people; he specifies the place of the captivity, Kir, but does not mention the nationality of the captors. Our historical records in 2 Kings xvi. 9 actually narrate the fulfilment of this prediction some half-century later—"the king of Assyria went up against Damascus and took it, and carried away the people of it captive to Kir, and slew Resin." But we certainly must not make our conception of 'inspired prophecy' depend on a fact of this kind, unless we can be much more certain than we actually are of the relation which exists between the prophet and the historical book. That is to say, we must not put upon the same plane the great ethical inspiration which we have just examined and this prediction and fulfilment of a captivity of Damascus.

In a general way, again, we may affirm that Gaza, and Tyre, and Edom, Ammon and Moab fell under the ruin which the prophet predicts but we have no information of a specific kind and in the general cataclysms of subsequent history which wiped out most of the cities and peoples that were contemporaneous with Amos, we cannot detect any sure and definite sign of literal prophetic fulfilment. On the other hand, the vague prediction of Israel's own captivity was, as we know, strikingly fulfilled at the same time that Damascus fell. "The king of Assyria took Samaria, and carried Israel away into Assyria" (2 Kings xvii. 6). The very vagueness of the threat—the description of the captivity, for instance, as "beyond Damascus"—is an interesting evidence that it was written before the event, and actually uttered by Amos It would seem, if one may say so, that this indefinite and figurative language is a mark of genuine prediction; where details are given too minutely we usually detect indications that the apparent prophecy is in reality a narrative thrown into the past and put into the mouth of some historical person. The Apocryphal writings of later Judaism are full of such instances; and in no respect are they more strikingly marked off from the genuine prophets.

Amos, when he is foretelling the ruin of his country, does not attempt to go into details which were unknown to him, neither does he make any delusive show of accurate knowledge; but he gives one graphic and tragic picture of the distress which would prevail in the besieged city, and that picture is symbolical rather than literal. A man is lying dead in his house, where already all the other members of his family are dead; a distant kinsman therefore comes to give him the last rites of burial, and he asks, Is there yet any with thee? and from the secret recesses of the vacant dwelling comes a mysterious voice saying, No. The horrified kinsman proceeds with his mournful work in silence, exclaiming that there must be no mention made of Israel's God, who had thus fully and finally deserted His people (vi. 9, 10). About this there is all the passion and insight of the seer, but there is no attempt at detailed prediction. And if in foretelling the event which already in the Assyrian attack upon Damascus was casting its shadow before it, the prophet saw nothing but the vague and general and hopeless ruin, we need not be surprised that his forecasts of the future triumph of David's tabernacle (ix. 11) are kept within narrow forms and give but little sign that they are pointing to that far-off Divine event, the coming of the Kingdom of God in the truest sense.

After a careful study, then, of this one early prophet, we may sum up our conclusions in a sentence. We find that the inspiration of our prophet is to be recognized not so much in predicting definite future events, as in courageous God-directed testimony to the Eternal Law of Righteousness which is the will of God, in fearless denunciation against his own nation which had violated the law, and in assurance that no privilege of birth or election could in the least avail to avert the penalty which follows upon its violation.

This is only one of the prophets. There are eleven other minor ones, so-called. There are also the four great books which are collected under the respective names of Isaiah, Jeremiah, Ezekiel, and Daniel. If we were proceeding by any other way than that of suggestion and illustration, it would be incumbent on us to subject each one of these to such an examination as this to which we have subjected Amos. That is a long and laborious, but an absorbingly interesting, task. In the case of the larger books more especially, the question of authorship becomes complicated, because it was a habit of the literary compilers and editors of the Second Temple to bring together "oracles" and "prophecies" and publish them under one great name, without wishing to authoritatively declare that they all proceeded from the one great person. Thus in a book like Isaiah we cannot without inquiry assume that all the prophecies were even supposed to have come from Isaiah himself. When a careful examination of the whole is made, it quickly appears that the book consists of two distinct parts which differ from one another in style and subject and spirit. From chapter xl. onwards we seem to be dealing with quite another author. No preconceived theories must make us determine that the authorship is different; but, on the other hand, we must quietly and calmly look the facts in the face, and allow them to tell upon us. If the clear facts force us to the conclusion that while some parts of the book were written by Isaiah, the contemporary of Hezekiah, other parts were written by other hands unknown, we are then to allow this conclusion to take its place in our conception of a prophetic book, and not to make the verities of God even seem to be dependent upon a disputed authorship. Again, in the case of Daniel we are met by very difficult and serious problems. The solution of these problems is by no means generally accepted. For a long time it was supposed a part of the Christian Faith to maintain that the book was written by Daniel in Babylon. Accordingly it was maintained with considerable ability and zeal, and even with not a little heat and violence. But now we see more clearly that a question lay behind that, the answer to which had been quietly assumed. That question was whether it was in the remotest degree necessary to maintain the authorship of Daniel, if we wished to profess and call ourselves Christians. Clearly it was not. Thenceforward we began, not to set up a more or less skilful defence of the traditional authorship, but to ask earnestly and diligently to what the facts point. Now it can hardly be denied, when prejudice is quite laid aside, that the facts point to a very clear conclusion, viz., that the Book of Daniel is one of a class, and differs in quality rather than in kind from other works of the same class—a class of writings which sprang up in the days of the national resistance to Antiochus Epiphanes. It was characteristic of this class of works to appear under the name of some distinguished personality, Enoch, Moses, the Patriarchs, and so on. There was no intention to deceive, any more than Milton wished to deceive when he put some of the noblest thoughts that have ever been uttered into the mouths of the persons in " Paradise Lost." The faithful servants of God, who were resisting the blasphemous tyranny of Antiochus, were strengthened in their noble struggle by the glowing stories and marvellously beautiful visions which had marked the life of the great Daniel in Babylon. Now if this prove to be the origin of the book, it would indeed be blindness to shut our eyes to the fact in the interest of a perfectly unauthorized theory. That the Inspired Book should contain, among its wonderfully rich variety of contents, this noble specimen of what is called Pseudepigraphical literature, need not surprise us: on the contrary, we should then have a light thrown upon that intensely interesting part of Jewish history, about which it is generally supposed that the Bible is silent, the period when the noble fervour, the singleness of heart, and the passionately pure monotheism which had been learnt in the sorrow of captivity, made the Jewish people, under the Hasmonean dynasty, greater than they had ever been in the brilliant days of the undivided monarchy. In any case, all that we need contend for is that the right view of Inspiration will not hinder us from facing the facts in a case of disputed authorship like this, but rather will hold itself ready to accept and take account of the conclusion when it is reached, ready also to admit the uncertainty in case a conclusion cannot be reached.

And now supposing, instead of leaving a great gap which can only be filled by a minute study of all the Prophets—supposing we had actually gone through them all as we have gone through Amos, to what conclusion would the investigation point? We should find that every prophet has an individuality of his own, and every prophet is largely explained by the circumstances of his time. But we should find, if a little dogmatism may be allowed to stand provisionally where the gap yawns unfilled, that there is a remarkable unity in the Prophets; they all have the same intense Ethical life; they all point forward to a completer realization of moral peace and joy than has ever been experienced in any mythical age of Gold. They all have visions—visions shaped more or less by the circumstances and conditions of their own lives—visions of the way in which this consummation is to be reached, and of the form which it is to take. They all connect the beautiful predictions of the future with the Israel of which they formed a part—they all see that through tribulation and chastisement, national ruin, and national restoration, Israel was to be the instrument rather than the object of the fulfilment of their predictions. Before the eyes of some, Israel, the chastened, imperfect, disciplined, failing Servant of God, assumed a new and strange significance. Out of it came a Person, a Servant, a King, a Branch, a Root. From these searchings of the prophets grew that great idea of a Messiah, or Christ, which meets us in the most pronounced shape in the days of our Lord. Prophecy at its highest point is concerned with the New Order which is to come in with this personal King. In imagery, sometimes prosaic, sometimes exquisitely, passionately poetical; sometimes vague and fitful, sometimes distinct and clear and strong like a great and perfect piece of music; sometimes so immeshed in the circumstances of the time that it cannot be disentangled, sometimes soaring quite above all local and temporal conditions; the Kingdom of God is portrayed and foretold. So grand and unmistakable is the general Prediction, so free and bold are the general outlines, that sometimes we have been tempted to press details and to rest the case of Prophecy and its fulfilment upon verbal predictions, which often turn out to be little better than quibbles. But this misuse of prophecy does not affect its use. It was the great God-given discipline in the very centre of Israel by which Israel developed into the Kingdom of God, and David's throne and Aaron's priesthood were enlarged into the throne and priesthood of Christ.

CHAPTER VI.

OF THE HISTORY IN THE INSPIRED BOOK.

In the Old Testament we have a history or histories of that remarkable people of Israel, which, as we have seen, was the prototype of the Kingdom of God. The connection of Israel with Christianity and indeed the quite unique position of the Jews in the present day, would, apart from all other considerations, lead us to attach an extraordinary importance to the early history of a nation which has played and still plays so singular a part in the world. Facing the broad facts, before we turn to any records at all we are impelled to say, "There is about this people something which marks them off from all other peoples; it is a miraculous people, in the sense that it is a wonder and astonishment unto many; it is an inspired people, in the sense that its national utterance, its literature, has a universal Divine significance, and its national life culminates in a Person whom we cannot but regard as the centre of humanity." Bunsen used to say that as long as the Jews existed in their present marked position amongst men,

Divine revelation could never be wanting in a witness. That we feel to be true. Now supposing—it is of course a far-fetched supposition—that no historical records of Israel's origin had survived; supposing this people had emerged on the plane of history at the time when they came into contact with the Roman armies under Pompeius; still, on the strength of that spiritual force which came from them at the beginning of our era and changed the whole face of Europe, creating the modern world, and on the strength of the characteristics of the people preserved in the broad light of history during nineteen hundred years, we should be forced to conjecture that the origin, veiled in obscurity, must have been in all ways remarkable. In vain should we have sought to derive an explanation from a study of Semitic history or Semitic literature; the vanished Babylonian and the surviving Arab would in vain be interrogated to discover how their kinsman of the tiny strip of country in the south-east corner of the Mediterranean had occupied this unique position in human history. Possibly even in our utter ignorance of the antecedents of the Nation we should have said conjecturally, "They must have been trained by the Divine mind, taught by the Divine discipline, instructed in some way or other by the Divine voice: God has not dealt so with any nation." This, surely, every writer, speaking with any inner knowledge of the Divine mystery of the Christian life and faith, would have instinctively said; and even "rationalist" historians, as they are called, speaking without that key to history which the knowledge of Christ supplies, would have been, as indeed they still are, sorely puzzled to explain the stubborn fact submitted to them.

Thus, apart from an examination of the historical records, before we even approach them, we are prepared for something out of the common; unless we can find something out of the common we shall be left with an effect on our hands lacking a sufficient cause. If we may put it in a bold and almost startling form, we are convinced of the inspired character of the nation before we examine in detail the nation's history, and we are prepared from the outset to give a special name, to ascribe a special attribute, to the records of a people which has been guided and taught by a special Divine discipline. This special name, this special attribute, is very generally agreed to be Inspiration. The history of Israel is *inspired;* that being assumed, or rather ascertained, from the broad survey of facts, we have to turn and inquire as carefully as our limits will permit what is the content which must be given to Inspiration in this connection; what are the marks, the phenomena, of the inspired histories?

At once we are met with a startling fact. Just as in the Biography of the New Testament we had two distinct narratives (viz., the Synoptic and the Johannine), so in the History of the Old Testament we have two distinct narratives, covering to some extent the same ground. Taking historical excerpts from the first six books of the Bible, and then going on in a continuous narrative from the beginning of Judges to the end of the Second Book of Kings, we have a story—true, a story with many gaps in it—still a connected story from the earliest times to the captivity of Judah. Then starting from the First Book of Chronicles, and reading on to the end of Nehemiah, we have, in a very compressed form, though enlarged in some parts, a complete record from Adam to the return from captivity; at the end of this long sweep of narrative comes the Book of Esther, which is a brief appendix containing a historical episode of the Captivity. Taking these two distinct histories, we have two parallel lines of narrative, an older and a later, which run together up to the time of the Captivity: the older, though covering a shorter time, is much the longer and fuller; the later, very thin in most parts, becomes very full in its account of the Temple worship and Temple kingship at Jerusalem, and then continues the story alone up to the end of the Captivity and the re-establishment of the Temple worship after the return. In face of this double and partly parallel narrative, preconceived theories of what inspired history ought to be must be surrendered. The first duty should be to examine the two stories side by side, in order to discover whether they are in complete agreement. If it should appear that in certain respects discrepancies or divergences are discoverable, then we must take care not to lay stress on the accuracy of similar statements in cases where the narrative is not double but single. It would almost seem as if the Inspired Book had given us these duplicate narratives expressly to call our attention to the degree of accuracy in detail which we are entitled to expect in Inspired History. Sometimes we have been inclined to insist on a faultless correctness in the Biblical records which the Bible itself implicitly labours to repudiate. It tells us the same story twice in different language and with different colouring, in order that we may not rest in the form or in the letter, but learn to apprehend the substance.

It will help us to get a clear idea of the problem before us if we try to fix the dates, so far as that may be possible, of our two histories. The last event mentioned in the Second Book of Kings is in the first year of the reign of Evil-merodach, king of Babylon, that is 561 B.C. We may conclude then that the History as we have it was written after that year: but it must have been written before the return under Zerubbabel in 538 B.C., or else some reference to that great event would be made. It is fairly clear, therefore, that the History, which we have called the Older History, took shape in Babylon about the middle of the sixth century before Christ. For simplicity's sake let us set the date at 555 B.C.

The second, or as we have called it the Later

History allows us to determine its date with some approach to accuracy, for in i. Chron. iii. 19 the genealogy is carried on for six generations after the captives' return. This is, of course, not very determinate, but it would carry us down at least to 355 B.C.; it might be later, it might be as late as 300 when Hodaviah, Eliashib, Pelaiah, and the rest of them, were the living representatives of Zerubbabel's family (i. Chron. iii. 24). But for our purpose it is enough to say that about two hundred years intervene between the two histories; the Older belongs to the sixth, and the Later to the fourth century before our era. The writer or compiler of the Older was already removed from Samuel by at least six hundred years, a space of time as long as that which separates us from the first Parliament under Edward the First. The writer or compiler of the Later stood in about the same chronological relation to David as that in which Professor Freeman stands to William Rufus. It is necessary sometimes to interspace, if we may so term it, the Biblical records; for having the whole in one small volume, there is a constant danger of regarding everything as on precisely the same historical plane.

Having, then, marked in time our two Histories we may compare them together. It is at once apparent that the Later draws upon the earlier, but does not feel bound by it. The later has a way of increasing the numbers which occur in the earlier, adding a certain pomp and circumstance to its descriptions; and again and again it gives another tone to the narrative: it is as if it were telling the tale with a motive, with a practical application which it wishes to make. It distinctly refers to the earlier narrative (ii. Chron. xx. 34), though it does not tell us what degree of importance is to be attached to it; from the many deviations, or alterations, it would seem to regard itself as occupying a free and independent position with regard to its predecessor. We notice, too, that in the early part of our history where the writer is dealing with facts which happened many centuries before, there is a certain want of historical vividness; it often gives one the same impression as facts quoted in a sermon with a didactic purpose; the stress seems to be not on the facts, but on the inference or the instruction which is to be drawn from them.

In i. Chron. x., to give an example, a quotation is made from i. Samuel xxxi.; it is a description of the battle on Mount Gilboa. When, however, we come to verse 6 there is a variation. The Older History tells us with great simplicity that "Saul died, and his three sons, and his armour-bearer, and all his men;" the Later says, "his three sons, and all *his house*, died together." This is the more striking because in chapter ix. 40-44 the writer has just given us a genealogy of Saul's "house" through the line of Jonathan. Perhaps it may be well to give some further illustrations of the changes which are made in details.

In the Older History, ii. Samuel v. 21, we read that David smote the Philistines and called the name of the place *Baal-perazim*, "And they left their images there, and David and his men took them away." Our Later narrative (i. Chron. xiv. 12), as if fearing lest it might seem that David had carried away the images in order to use them in worship, says, "David gave commandment, and they were burned with fire." We may here mention other slight variations which give us a clue to the freedom of the writers. In ii. Samuel viii. 4 we read that David took from the king of Zobah "a thousand and seven hundred horsemen"; curiously enough, this appears in i. Chron. xviii. 4, "a thousand *chariots* and seven *thousand* horsemen." In the eighteenth chapter of i. Chron., verse 8 shows an addition, verse 12 a change, and verse 17 a curious suppression, as compared with the corresponding verses in Samuel. The curious suppression is this: our Later authority will not have it that the sons of David were "priests," and the Older authority says that they were. In chapter xx., verses 1 and 3, we have a glimpse into the nature of compilation. In verse 1 it says "David tarried in Jerusalem," in verse 3 that David returned to Jerusalem. The writer has omitted to mention that David was summoned to Rabbah (*vid.* ii. Sam. xii. 29).

In i. Chron. xxi. 1 there is a striking dogmatic correction of the Older narrative, which deserves a careful notice. The Older narrative says "The anger of the Lord was kindled against Israel, and he moved David against them, saying, Go, number Israel and Judah" (ii. Sam. xxiv. 1). The Later narrative, not liking to ascribe the suggestion to God, says that it came from Satan. We could hardly have a clearer instance of the freedom with which one writer deals with an older narrative; and, duly understood, this example may give us a most valuable hint in interpreting many passages where the style of Israelitic thought attributes actions or thoughts of men directly to God's suggestion. A more insignificant, but yet striking, variation is found in the numbers of the people as returned in the census of David. In ii. Samuel xxiv. 9 Israel is reckoned at 800,000 warriors, and Judah at 500,000. In i. Chron. xxi. 5 the return is 1,100,000 for Israel, and 470,000 for Judah. If we follow the parallel narratives of the events connected with the numbering, we find the Later giving several heightening touches (cf. verses 16, 20, 26). The most startling exaggeration, however, is in the price which David paid for the threshing-floor. This, in ii. Samuel xxiv. 24, is 50 shekels of silver, in i. Chron. xxi. 24, 600 *shekels of gold.* It almost looks as if the later authority had thought David's acknowledgment insufficient, and had wished to present the great king's generosity in a larger light.

In chapter xxiii. of our book it is worth noticing the part which the priests and Levites play, for they are not mentioned in the parallel place of the Older narrative. It would seem that the arrangements of Priestly and Levitical functions ascribed to David by the writer of the fourth century B.C., were not ascribed to him, or known as in any special way connected with him, by the writer of the sixth century B.C. In chap. xxviii., again, there is a startling addition to the Older narrative; at verse 19 David says that he had received the plan of the Temple and its appurtances *in writing* from God Himself.

It would take us much too far afield to go through all the variations between our two narratives. The opening chapters of ii. Chronicles are, however, too interesting to be passed over. Quite a different colour is given to the Older narrative; there seems to be a wish to set the events in a new light. In i. Kings iii. 3, 4 Solomon is charged with sacrificing in the high places, and Gibeon is represented as the chief of the high places. But the Chronicler (ii. Chron. i. 3) informs us that the Tabernacle was kept at Gibeon, though the Ark was kept at Jerusalem. The passage, ii. Chron. ii. 4, has nothing to represent it in the narrative of Samuel. The magnificence of Solomon is set in a dazzling light when the "twenty measures of pure oil" promised to Hiram (i. Kings v. 11) appear as "20,000 baths" ($=$2,000 measures), besides the doubled quantity of grain and the 20,000 baths of wine. Again, the Older narrative said that the levy of workers for the temple was raised out of Israel (i. Kings v. 13); the Later says these workers were "strangers" (ii. Chron. ii. 17). It would almost seem as if the later Israelites resented the impression that their own ancestors had with their own hands done the work.

The description of the Temple again offers some significant divergences. Compare especially chapters iii. 4, 11, 15; iv. 1, 5, 7; v. 4, with the corresponding places in Kings. What, we may ask, is meant by the change in ii. Chron. v. 4, compared with i. Kings viii. 3? In the earlier narrative the "priests" carry the ark; in the later this comparatively menial function is performed by the "Levites."

Other changes may be noted in ii. Chron. vi. 39; vii. 1-12; viii. 10-18; xi. 16; xiii. 9, 10; xiv. 5-9; xxi. 11, 12; xxii. 2; xxiii. 2; xxviii. 16, &c. One very inexplicable change may be more closely specified. In ii. Chron. viii. 2 we read of cities which Huram had given to Solomon, being built and occupied by Israelites. This seems as if it directly reversed the statement of i. Kings ix. 11, which tells us that it was Solomon who gave twenty cities to Hiram in return for the services the Syrian king had rendered in the building of the Temple. Are we to say that there had been an exchange of cities? Or are we to conclude that the Chronicler did not like to admit that the great King Solomon had actually surrendered cities on Israelite soil to an alien king?

We must, however, be content to leave this comparison between the sixth-century history and the fourth-century recasting of the narrative, without carrying it out into details ; nor is it necessary just now to explain the deviations by suggesting a motive for them. It is enough to observe that the deviations exist, that they are pretty numerous, if not very important; that they are sometimes to be found in details, sometimes in the general tone and colour given to the narrative ; and that they must have been quite deliberate, because the Later writer had the Older history before him.

It is clear, then, that we have only two courses before us ; either we must reject the one history in favour of the other, giving the preference to the Older as written nearer the events, or to the Later as serving a more didactic purpose; or, retaining both, we must admit into our idea of Inspired History a large latitude in dealing with facts and in furnishing details. It is hardly necessary to say that this second alternative is the one which accords with the view taken in the present book. If we may venture to look at our Inspired Histories from the standpoint of an Overruling Spirit directing their composition, we should say that the Spirit has carefully warned us against an undue stress upon details, an undue regard to the mere letter of history, by giving us side by side *two* narratives which are by no means in complete agreement with one another ; and thus we are almost compelled to take a broader view, to study the story in mass and in general outline ; and furthermore to recognize that Inspired History does not seek, like modern critical and scientific history, to render an exact and minute account of the events, but rather to present the main lines of God's dealings with men and of His purpose for the nation whose history is being recounted.

We must now turn to a closer examination of the Older History itself, ignoring, for the time being, its relation to its much later successor. We ask, What can be known concerning its authorship and its composition? What is the light in which its narratives are to be regarded? What degree of insistence does it permit us to lay upon the details? In a word, What is this History?

We have spoken of the Older narrative hitherto as if it were a single composition coming from the pen of one author. This, however, was only for the convenience of comparing it with the Later narrative. Actually, it is divided into many sections, which are called by different names. It would be a long and laborious process to accurately distinguish and arrange these sections. The difficulty of the task may be hinted at in an illustration; the narrative of Joshua of course precedes the narrative of Judges, but it seems very plain that the *Book* of Joshua is a later work than the *Book* of Judges. This will strike even a very casual reader; for in Joshua xxi. 43-45 we have the picture of Israel in happy possession of the conquered land—" There stood not a man of all their enemies before them; the Lord delivered all their enemies into their hand." If we are reading straight on from Joshua to Judges under the impression that it is a connected narrative, we must be taken aback to find all the Israelites "after the death of Joshua" engaged in a vigorous warfare against the inhabitants of the land. For instance, we read in Joshua x. 33 that Horam, king of Gezer, had been smitten, and he and his people utterly destroyed; in Judges i. 29 we are told that the Canaanites were still dwelling in Gezer unsubdued. But indeed the whole history of the Book of Judges presupposes a social and political condition which can hardly be reconciled with the picture given at the end of Joshua.

We are bound, then, to draw a line of demarcation between the Hexateuch,—if we may use the word which is now generally employed to designate the first six books of the Bible,—and the series of books which begins with Judges and ends with the Second Book of Kings. Leaving on one side the Hexateuch, we may perhaps further simplify our inquiry by passing over Judges and Ruth for the present. We come in this way to a fairly connected and unified work which is sometimes called the Four Books of Kings, and sometimes the Books of Samuel and the Books of the Kings.

A little examination of these four "Books" reveals that they are in reality only two. The division of the first two into the First and the Second of Samuel is quite artificial, for there is no break of a more decided nature than the break between two connected chapters in a modern book. The division between the First and the Second of Kings is even more artificial, and can only be justified by the convenience of use and reference, especially in the days when a volume was a parchment roll of cumbersome dimensions. On the other hand, Samuel and Kings are quite distinct. Their narratives may be pieced together, but the difference of style and treatment is quite enough to make us sure that the writer of one was not the writer of the other. It will therefore be necessary to examine the two separately. We shall take the Book of Samuel as a whole, and then we shall take the Book of Kings as a whole; and only when we have looked at both shall we attempt to draw any conclusions concerning the history which they contain.

Can we fix the authorship of the Book of Samuel? There is absolutely no internal evidence to help us; the author is entirely self-suppressive. Equally useless is any inference which might be drawn from the traditional idea that Samuel is the author. In fact, it must always be regarded as one of the most striking instances of easy-going traditionalism in matters of Biblical study, where the judgment is hushed into a submissive silence, that the book before us should ever have been ascribed to Samuel. There is no sign that the author of the first part is not the author of the second; and yet Samuel is dead and buried even before the end of the first part, and therefore certainly could not have touched the second. The story of Samuel is the connecting link between the time of the Judges and the monarchy; it occupies the opening chapters of our book. Tradition therefore, with an easy assurance, supposed that Samuel was the author; just as a reader of Macaulay's history, reading with the same level of critical intelligence which is often brought to bear in Biblical study, might in the absence of the title-page conclude that William of Orange wrote the book because he plays a prominent part in the story. No, we must be content to remain in ignorance about the author; for conjectures, such as the one we have been looking at, or the other, that Nathan and Gad wrote in continuation of Samuel's work, are not only baseless, they are positively harmful, because they tend to obscure the fact that in the Inspired Histories of the Old Testament the question of authorship is not to be considered important. The same remark must be made about the date of composition. It is natural to suppose that it was written soon after the events recorded in its closing pages, viz., the numbering of the people and the consequent plague which was sent as a punishment. But the point which we are now going to take into account leads us to conclude that the book as we have it is a much later compilation, and may even have to be referred to the time just preceding the Captivity.

While we can say nothing about author or date, we can very confidently affirm that the author in writing it used pre-existing historical materials and not only so, but used them in the way that was common before the dawn of a critical method in historical composition.

The two facts upon which we shall now dwell for a moment, giving such illustrations as space will permit, may be stated thus: (1) The author had authorities before him which he had studied and sought to follow; (2) His authorities were not always in harmony with each other, and consequently his attempt to combine them into a single narrative was not always quite successful.

The author had historical records before him. There is reason to think that the art of writing which the Greeks learnt from the Phœnicians was familiar to the Israelites from the very earliest times, and that the habit of composing national songs, proverbs, brief annals, &c., was encouraged by the leaders of the people, who took pains to preserve the compositions for the use of those that should come after. Of this practice we get an illustration in i. Samuel x. 25, "Then Samuel told the people the manner of the kingdom, and wrote it in a book, and laid it up before the Lord." The discovery of Egyptian writings, such as the poem of Pentaur, in our own day, writings which date from centuries before the time of Samuel, has reminded the modern world of the literary culture which existed in the Eastern Mediterranean two thousand years and more before our Northern nations received the first elements of letters. Samuel wrote a book containing the transactions of his own day. And, "laid up before the Lord" in the House of the Lord at Shiloh, and at other sanctuaries, were, we may be sure, numbers of similar documents. In i. Chron. xxix. 29 we have a reference to the "history of Samuel the seer, and the history of Nathan the prophet, and the history of Gad the seer;" and though we could hardly quote a book of the fourth century B.C. as very direct evidence to the literary authenticity of books written six hundred years before, still we may be quite satisfied that historical records, narrating contemporary events, were regular products of Israelite life in the olden times; so that when the author of the book before us sat down to compose his work he would have ample materials to draw upon. A compilation from contemporary documents is the best idea of history that we can form; and this is precisely what, it would seem, figures largely in this history.

There is one book of those early days to which reference is made, and from which quotations are taken, more than once in our historical books. It seems to have been a collection of songs. Every great nation, in its heroic age, has its songs, which commemorate the battle in tuneful verse, or wail with lyrical passion over the tragedies of the national life. Israel was no exception to the rule: and in very remote antiquity these folk-songs gained a literary form and were collected in a volume, the name of which was "The Book of Jashar." We may conjecture that the Song of Deborah, that earliest and most authentic folk-song of Israel, had a place in this book. We are expressly told that the source from which the author of the Book of Joshua drew his account of the great battle at Gibeon was a song in this book (Josh. x. 13), and a fragment of the poem is actually quoted. The author of the Book of Samuel made use of the song-book too: he gives us a quotation from it, that exquisite threnody of David over the death of Saul and Jonathan his son (ii. Sam. i. 18–27). It would not perhaps be difficult to distinguish many of the stirring episodes in the book, which move with a life and passion all their own, as having their source in these ballads and lyrics of contemporary poets.

Thus our author allows us to guess with some certainty at his method of composition. He took the records written by leaders of the people, such as the prophets Samuel, Nathan, and Gad, or by any other chroniclers who wrote with the authority of contemporaries. Out of these records he constructed his narrative, heightening its effect by carefully studying the folk-lore and the folk-songs, and thus breathing into his pages, sometimes by distant allusion, sometimes by direct quotation, all the fire and passion of the actors and eye-witnesses of the events. This leads us to notice the second fact which was just now pointed out, that sometimes he was puzzled by different accounts of the same event; and in trying to utilize his contradictory materials he is not always able to produce a smooth and harmonious narrative. But this fact only shows us the more clearly and significantly the method of composition. Two illustrations may be given. The first shall be from the story of Saul, the second from the story of David.

Now it would appear that two opposite views existed about the origin of the monarchy in Israel. On the one hand—and this was probably the contemporary view—the monarchy was always regarded as the distinct and deliberate ordinance of God: it was the symbol of national greatness; prophetic hopes always took the form of a restoration of David's throne. This view appears very decisively in Deut. xvii. 14-20, where, among the ordinances of the Law, provision is made for a king. This passage assumes as a matter of course that the king would be made when the nation should be settled in its new home, and it gives directions for the choice of the king and for the regulations of the throne. But another view of the monarchy also prevailed, a view which certainly seems as if it must have sprung up when the many inherent defects of the monarchy had shown themselves, and a longing for a more direct government by God had entered into the heart of Israel. According to this view, the appointment of a king had not been contemplated by God; when the people, dissatisfied with the prophetic government of

Samuel, demanded a king like the other nations, it was regarded as an apostasy from God, and at last the king was inflicted upon them almost as a penalty.

These two opposite conceptions found expression in the ancient literature which referred to the institution of the monarchy. The author of the Book of Samuel gives expression to both in a way which seems to suggest that he is weaving together the two different versions. If we read, first of all, i. Sam. ix., 1-16, xi., xiii., xiv., we have a clear and harmonious narrative, which represents the appointment of Saul (cf. ix. 16) as an act of God's loving-kindness. The whole narrative moves in a joyous strain: the king is anointed at God's bidding; immediately he vindicates his position by a great victory, and all the grumblers are silenced (xi. 15). But now if we read chap. viii., and then chap. x. 17 onwards, and chap. xii., especially verse 17, we get quite a different impression. Asking for a king is regarded as an act of great wickedness, so that it is not easy to see how the passage in Deut. xvii. 14 could be explained, if it were written before this time and was familiar to the people: they might very reasonably ask of Samuel, "Is it not written in the Law that we shall have a king? Wherein have we sinned?" The two versions of the event are blended together with some skill, so that it does not seem impossible to find in the narrative a reconciliation between them; but it can hardly be doubted that the author had before him two different accounts. This appears still more manifest in the instance we shall now take from the story of David.

Reading the account of David's introduction to Saul in i. Samuel xvi., we first of all hear of Samuel anointing David at Bethlehem; then at xvi. 18 David is brought before the king as not only " cunning in playing," but a " mighty man of valour and a man of war." He stands before Saul because he has found favour in the king's sight. Then in chap. xvii. we are surprised to meet with David as a mere shepherd lad coming up from the country to the army, slaying Goliath, and so being introduced to Saul for the first time. In fact, as he goes out to the combat Saul sends Abner to inquire who he is; and in consequence of this episode the young man is enlisted in the king's service. Now there cannot be any reasonable doubt that this confusion arises from the existence of two accounts of David's first introduction to Saul. According to the one, he was sought out in Saul's mental distress as a cunning player on the harp. According to the other, he attracted the king's attention by an act of heroic valour in the army. So distinct are these accounts, that even in the welded narrative it is quite easy to separate them. Read xvi. 14–23 and then go on at xviii. 6, and you see you have a straightforward narrative: the section xvii.–xviii. 5 appears plainly as a separate piece coming no doubt from a separate source. This interpolated section is one of the most conned and loved of Old Testament stories; but it is certainly very puzzling to find our author in chap. xxi. 19 informing us that Goliath of Gath was killed not by David at all, but by another Bethlehemite named Elhanan. The Chronicler (i. Chron. xx. 5) was as puzzled as we are, and took the liberty of altering the statement, saying that Elhanan slew not Goliath but his brother. That, however, is another question. Our only concern just now is to notice and acknowledge the existence of different authorities, which our author has tried to harmonize. It is interesting to observe that he preferred leaving them unharmonized to tampering in any way with the facts.

But now let us turn from the books of Samuel to the second half of the Historical Narrative which is before us. This is divided into two sections, or chapters as we should call them now, and the two chapters are called in our Bible the First and the Second Book of Kings. This work differs from the one we have just been considering in one respect: we are able, within very narrow limits, to fix the date of its composition. In a quite undesigned way the book itself fixes the date: for in its closing verses it tells us what happened to the captive king Jehoiachin in the first year of Evil-merodach's reign. Now Evil-merodach began to reign in 561 B.C. And as our author shows no sign of knowing anything after that year, it seems natural to suppose that he wrote in that year. At any rate he must have written between 561 B.C and the year 538, which is the date of Zerubbabel's return to Jerusalem, for we cannot imagine that he would have stopped short at the point of profound national depression, if he had already lived to see the first signs of the coming restoration.

We may be tolerably sure, then, that we have before us a writing which was composed about 450 years after the death of David; and if we would form a correct idea of the author's position in setting about his task, we might say it would be very much as if an author in the present day were to sit down to write in a thin volume of sixty or seventy octavo pages the history of the English monarchy from the death of Henry the Sixth to this present year. It is clear, then, that unless the writer received some very exceptional powers for his task he would be dependent upon such histories, annals, records, as were already existing, and he would be exposed to all the uncertainties of date and detail which historical sources always present. The general idea of Inspired History is that the writer did receive some exceptional powers, so that without referring to any documents he was enabled to set down the story, and without depending on any chronologies he was enabled to give all the dates with infallible accuracy. But when we come to quietly examine this History Book before us, it is quite plain that such an idea of Inspiration is without foundation; on the contrary, it is clear that the author laboriously employed the historical materials which were within his reach, very much as a modern historian might do, and further that he was as much puzzled by chronological difficulties as a modern historian frequently is. But before we go into a few details to illustrate these two points, we ought to ask the question, Who wrote the book? We may say at once that the author does not give us any clue to his identity. And as he keeps silence upon the point, we may conclude that it is not of any importance that we should know. Still a curious fact may be mentioned, which at any rate is suggestive. The most eminent man in Judah at the time when the Book must have been written was the prophet Jeremiah, and the closing chapter of our Book is almost identical with the closing chapter of the Book of Jeremiah. This fact is obviously susceptible of several explanations; either book may have taken the passage from the other, or both may have taken it from a current history book. Very little therefore can be inferred from the fact as to the authorship of the Kings. But it is at any rate conceivable that Jeremiah may have been the author. Suppose for a moment that he was. Jeremiah is one of the most remarkable, one of the most strikingly inspired, men in the whole history of Israel. To him, if to any one, might have been granted a power of writing a historical narrative without the toil of historical research, and exempt from the liability to historical error. If, then, we were to accept the tradition that Jeremiah composed the Book of Kings, the facts which we are now to notice would be all the more significant

The two points which are to be illustrated are these: (1) the employment of historical records in the composition of the book; and (2) the occurrence of errors, especially chronological errors, in the history.

To begin at the beginning, in writing the first eleven chapters on the reign of Solomon the author had before him a book which was called "The Acts of Solomon." This seems to have been a much fuller work than his own, so much fuller that in bringing his narrative of Solomon to an end (i. Kings xi. 41) he refers his readers to this authority, apparently well known and recognized, for an account of "all that he (Solomon) did, and his wisdom." In the time of the Chronicler, this literature of the reign of Solomon had considerably increased, and in the corresponding place of the Chronicles (ii. Chron. ix. 29) reference is made to "The History of Nathan the Prophet," "The Prophecy of Ahijah the Shilonite," and "The Visions of Iddo the seer concerning Jeroboam the son of Nebat"; but already in the fifth century B.C., there was a history of Solomon's reign from which the author of our book was able to draw the materials for his summary narrative.

Then for his history of Jeroboam the author had as his source the "Book of the Chronicles of the Kings of Israel" (i. Kings xiv. 19), and for his history of Rehoboam he had a corresponding "Book of the Chronicles of the Kings of Judah" (i. Kings xiv. 29). It is fair to presume that these historical works in the divided kingdoms ran right on to the Captivity; in fact, it is tolerably clear that a historiographer royal must have been constantly at work recording the events which were passing in the kingdom before his eyes. Thus our author in the whole course of his work would most probably have contemporary records to draw upon, though of course there must have been great varieties of excellence in this string of authorities, which would differ, very much as the volumes issued by the Master of the Rolls differ, from one another. And if our author was thus dependent on his predecessors, it is only natural to suppose that his work reflects their varying degrees of accuracy or fulness of detail; we must not be surprised if in times of national excitement or national disaster our records show some confusion and uncertainty, nor need we be surprised if in some parts of the book we notice a much clearer or more ordered narrative than in others. That is almost unavoidable in the composition of history; the authorities for one period enable us to reproduce it in rich fulness of circumstance, the authorities for another period give us only confused hints, from which a toilsome study and reconstruction will only succeed in producing a more or less probable narrative. It appears that the author of the Books of Kings experienced some of these difficulties of the historian. We may perhaps recognize another source from which the author drew in his account of King Jehoshaphat (i. Kings xxii.), though he himself does not mention it. The Chronicler (ii. Chron. xx. 34) actually says that the "History of Jehu, the son of Hanani," *is inserted* in the book of the kings of Israel. If the book of the kings of Israel is actually our own Book of Kings, then we may suppose that the author simply embodied Jehu's work in his own. But if the book of the kings is only one of those chronicles already referred to (i. Kings xiv. 19, 29), still it is clear that our author had the writings of this Jehu before him.

Another inference seems pretty plain in another part of our book. In reading straight through, it must strike us that the narrative of Elijah the Tishbite (i. Kings xvii.–xix. and xxi.) is of a different complexion from the rest. There is more colour in it, more graphic description, more richness of incident. The suggestion at once presents itself that here our author has got before him, not the annals of the kingdom, but the stories preserved in the Schools of the Prophets. And so, again, when we come to the part which Elisha plays in the narrative, we seem suddenly transferred from the point of view of the historiographer royal to that of the monastic chronicler of the acts of the prophets. We cannot, however, lay much stress upon this point, because it is an inference rather than an explicit statement of the author. But the facts already mentioned make it indisputable that we should recognize in the Book of Kings a historical composition based upon pre-existing works which are now lost to us.

Turning to the second point, the errors, especially of a chronological kind, which are very obvious on the surface of the book, we may take a curious phenomenon to serve as a transition from what has been said to what is now to be said. The author in summing up his account of Hezekiah (ii. Kings xviii. 5), commending his piety in keeping the commandments of the Lord, says, "after him was none like him among all the kings of Judah, nor among them that were before him." Later on, in summing up the reign of King Josiah (xxiii. 25), and commending his piety in turning to the Lord with all his heart and with all his soul, the author oddly enough says, "like unto him there was no king before him; neither after him arose there any like him." It looks as if the first passage had been quoted from an authority which gave Hezekiah the palm, and the second from another authority which gave Josiah the palm of piety. If this is not the explanation we can only suppose that the author uses the phrase as a *façon de parler*, and does not mean to lay any insistence on it. In either case the strange little repetition and consequent contradiction indicates for us certain limits which we must expect in the accuracy of particular phrases in the book we are examining.

But now a word or two must be said about the chronology. An accurate system of dating events seems so essential to the modern historical sense, that to deny accuracy of this kind to a work seems almost equivalent to destroying its value. Accordingly, the usual theory of Inspiration—which constantly gathers into its idea of an inspired writing all the merits and perfections which from time to time are recognized or demanded in other writings—emphatically maintains that an inspired writer must be faultlessly exact, guaranteed from all possibility of an error in the matter of dates. Apart from this *à priori* theory, however, coming to look at the actual facts, we are immediately struck by the almost entire absence of chronological exactness in these historical writings. The author does not even seem to have considered what his own chronological statements really signify, so that contradictions of the most glaring character occur. Quite at the beginning of the book, in the sixth chapter, he calls the fourth year of Solomon's reign the four hundred and eightieth after the Exodus. But if we add up the dates supplied in the other books which went before, we find that there would be more like five hundred and eighty years between the two dates; and we know from the New Testament how, in St. Paul's speech, the period from Joshua to Samuel alone is reckoned at 450 years. In fact, so completely irreconcilable is this statement with all the other dates suggested in the Scriptural reckonings, that some commentators propose to strike out the clause in this verse which reads, "in the four hundred and eightieth year after the children of Israel were come out of the land of Egypt"—which is certainly a very convenient way of improving the chronological reputation of our author. But even if we were to do this, his chronological reputation would still stand in rather a precarious condition, for this statement at the outset is simply an example of his general laxity in the matter of dates all through. If any one tries to lay down the dates of the two lines of kings of Israel and Judah from the notices contained in this book, he will quickly perceive that he is attempting to do what the author never attempted. The author seems to have been content, in dealing with an Israelite king, to give the date reckoned by the year of the reigning king in Judah just as he found it stated in the Israelite chronicles, and then to do the same in dealing with the dates of the kings of Judah with reference to the reigning king of Israel; but he did not consider whether the two chronicles harmonized. We may take some illustrations from the latter part of the work. Hoshea began to reign in Israel (ii. Kings xv. 30) in *the twentieth year* of Jotham the king of Judah. So far writes our author, following the records of the Northern kingdom. For his next paragraph he turns to his records of the Southern kingdom, and naïvely tells us that Jotham never reached a twentieth year, but only reigned sixteen years (ver. 33): but even this is not the end of the difficulty; in chapter xvii. he goes back to the Northern kingdom, and tells us that Hoshea began to reign not in Jotham's reign at all, but in the reign of Ahaz, Jotham's successor; and if now he had said "in the fourth year of Ahaz," we might see our way through the perplexity, for the fourth year of Ahaz would at any rate be twenty years from the beginning of Jotham's reign, though Jotham himself had died after reigning sixteen years; but he says, not in the fourth, but "in the twelfth year of Ahaz, king of Judah." We may give it up, and exclaim, with the Speaker's commentator, "The chronological confusion of the history, as it stands, is striking!"—and then perhaps we may exclaim at the Speaker's commentator, that he and the like of him have given us so little account of these unmistakeable phenomena, and the cause of them, in the History.

One other illustration may suffice. King Ahaz, according to our authority, lived twenty years, and then came to the throne and reigned for sixteen years (ii. Kings xvi. 2). At his death, therefore, Ahaz was thirty-six years of age. In that year he was succeeded by his son Hezekiah, who was twenty-five years of age (ch. xviii. 2). This would mean that King Ahaz was married at the age of ten, which, making all allowance for the earlier puberty of Eastern boys, does not seem very probable; and the explanation is much more likely to be found in the chronological inaccuracies of our author, to which, if we have been observantly reading his book through, we shall by this time have become quite accustomed.

In a word, it is abundantly clear that whatever we may mean by Inspired History we at least must not include in the idea that kind of chronological exactness which we require in modern historical works; and when we have duly pondered the facts which have just been mentioned, we shall feel indeed an indescribable amazement in hearing—as we may any day hear if we choose—pious persons maintaining that "when God writes history He will be at least as accurate as Bishop Stubbs or Mr. Gardiner; and if we are to admit errors in His historical work, then why not in His plan of salvation and doctrine of atonement?" Could any argument, we may ask, be more calculated to produce a widespread doubt concerning God's "plan of salvation and doctrine of atonement"?

But it is time to draw to a head this somewhat lengthened discussion of the Historical Books and to see if it has given us any help in forming a clearer conception of what we mean by their inspiration.

We have seen, broadly speaking, that, regarded as historical compositions, they show the marks of an origin similar to that of most other ancient historical works. The writers, writing centuries after the events, rely upon existing records which were more or less contemporaneous with the things recorded in them. Using these historical materials, very much as historians use materials still, the historian endeavoured to extract from them a uniform and consistent narrative; but his endeavour is seldom quite successful, for a careful study of his books constantly reveals discrepancies which are best explained by recognizing a combination of different sources. We have seen that these writings are by no means faultlessly correct; that, without travelling outside the Bible itself to find other authorities, we are able to detect quite palpable errors, especially in the matter of chronology, in the books themselves. From all this we are bound to infer that Inspired History is not history which in its method of composition and infallibility of detail is marked off from other Ancient History.

Where then, we may ask, are we to look for its Inspiration? The answer can only be hinted at here; but if we attentively consider what we actually mean by Inspiration in such a connection, we shall find that it is not in any material degree affected by the conclusions to which we have been forced. *It is not the historical record so much as the history itself that is inspired.* The inspiration is to be sought in the story of the chosen people, and the inspiration therefore breathes in these books just in proportion as they enable us to understand the course and direction of that story. Apart altogether from the books, the story, so far as it may be inferred from the existence of the Jews at the present day and from the Christian Faith which had its roots in Judaism, bears the marks of Inspiration; and sometimes we are more conscious of the inspiration when we are surveying the broad facts than when we are tracing the more or less trustworthy details in these ancient books. The story moves in a grand and unmistakeable curve: it tells us how the chosen people took to themselves a king; how the kingdom suddenly bloomed into goodness and greatness under David and Solomon, leaving an ideal which the nation could never surrender; it tells us how, first by the grand schism, and then by ever-increasing outbreaks of sin and disloyalty, the nation dwindled in lamentable decadence and finally vanished in captivity, leaving, as it seemed, the Ideal of the Kingdom as a golden glory in the past, and yet throwing it forward in the darkest days of desolation as a golden hope for the future. It is therefore a detailed story of a noble hope, a gathering despair, and a larger hope rising above despair. As such, this story holds its necessary place in the Divine Revelation of the Kingdom of God. Not so much for the value of the detailed events, as for the implied prophecy in the whole, it assumes a peculiar and Divine significance: and as a wonderful and illuminated example of the way in which the Divine wisdom is ordering and controlling the events of History, it becomes in a manner a key to the interpretation of uninspired history.

Is there, then, it will be said, no inspired element in the actual writing? Is it, after all, only the ordinary record of an extraordinary history? And an answer may be given. Whoever these unknown authors were, and we have seen that the historical books which we have examined are all anonymous, we may say of them generally, apart from the indications in the quoted authorities, that they were prophets and sons of the prophets. Indifferent as they were to historical consistency and chronological accuracy, they were keenly alive to the element of revelation in the events they were narrating; they, perhaps unconsciously, selected their materials, and arranged them in a didactic, an almost homiletical, way. It seems as if their purpose was not so much to tell us what happened, as to emphasize for us the lesson of what happened. It is applied history, rather than history pure and simple; and on this ground we can understand that tendency to irritation which critical historians sometimes betray in approaching it. It is then, if we may so put it, history written in the prophetic method. And this remark, duly considered, explains both the defects and the unique merits of the historical books of the Old Testament. On the one hand it explains the indifference to details. The prophetic historian would never dream, like a modern scientific historian, of writing interminable monographs about a disputed name, or an uncertain date; he might even take a story which rested on very doubtful authority, finding in it more that would suit his purpose than the bare and accurate statement of the fact which could be authenticated. The standpoint of the prophetic historian and that of the scientific historian are wholly different: they cannot be judged by the same canons of criticism.

On the other hand the above distinction explains the element which, we instinctively feel, marks this history off from ordinary history. To the prophetic eye the significance of all events seems to be in their relation to the will of God. The prophet may not always discern what the will of God is: he may interpret events in a quite inadequate manner. But his predominant thought makes itself felt; and consequently the study of these histories leaves us in a widely different frame of mind from that which Thucydides or Mr. Freeman would produce. We do not feel to know, perhaps, so accurately about the wars between Israel and Judah as we do about the wars between Athens and Sparta; we do not feel to know, perhaps, so much about the monarchy of Israel as we know about the Anglo-Norman monarchy; but on the other hand we seem to be more aware of God, we seem to recognize His hand controlling the wavering affairs of states, we seem to comprehend that obedience to His will is of more importance than any political consideration, and that in the long course of History disobedience to His will means national distress and national ruin. The story of scientific histories has its advantages; but it is not quite certain that those advantages are greater than those which the study of prophetic history yields. Perhaps, after all, *the one fact* of History is God's work in it; in which case the scientific histories, with all their learning and with all their toil, will look rather small by the side of these imperfect compositions which at least saw vividly and recognized faithfully *the one fact*.

And thus making due allowance for all the facts which candour has required and may yet require us to recognize, we shall not be left in much doubt concerning the inspiration of these books. Our idea of Inspiration may have been changed; it will not have been lessened.

CHAPTER VII.

THE LAW.

At the beginning of the Bible occur five—perhaps we ought to say six—brief works which seem to form a compact whole. This Book, if we may treat it as a book by itself, gives a historical sketch which embraces many hundreds of years. First of all it tells about this origin of Man in the Creation, then it narrows its subject to the origin of Israel, and then it traces the history of this one people, taking less and less notice of the outside nations, up to the time when the land of the Canaanites has been possessed and subdued. Interwoven with this historical narrative we find a series of laws or regulations for the civil and religious ordering of this one people. The names we give to the six divisions which form this book at once remind us that our view of their literary composition is not a primitive, but a comparatively recent, one. We call four of the books by *Greek* names, viz., Genesis, Exodus, Leviticus, Deuteronomy, and one of them by a Latin name, viz., Numbers. This shows us that we are not following any early Hebrew designation, but only the titles or headings which were adopted when the Greek version made its appearance not long before the Christian era. And indeed in the Hebrew these names are quite unknown; the several books or divisions of the work are simply called by the first word of the book or division.

We have just noticed that the sixth book, the Book of Joshua, seems to form quite an integral part of this treatise which is called by the Greek name, Pentateuch, or Five Volumes; but in the discussion in which we are now engaged we may perhaps more conveniently set it aside, and simply look at the Five Books; for at the time when we first begin to perceive the Canon of the Old Testament Scriptures assuming a definite shape, these Five Books are treated as a separate work, entitled the Law. Even when the books of the Chronicles were compiled, about 300 years before Christ, this Law was referred to as a single whole (see ii. Chron. xxv. 4, xxxv. 12).

It needs hardly to be said that the Jewish people, as they appear to us in the times after the exile, and especially in the familiar pages of the New Testament, attached a unique importance to this Law. Regarding their Sacred Books as divisible into three groups, the Prophets (which included the Histories), the Hagiographa, and the Law, they set the Law in a place by itself, a place of unapproachable dignity and authority. It is to this fact that the Law owes the position it takes in our Bible to this day, and not to any trustworthy determination of a prior date which could be urged as prejudicing a free inquiry as to its origin. We are constantly tempted to accept in an unquestioning spirit these dispositions of the Synagogue, and to deem it almost a sacrilege to cast a suspicion on anything which was settled and accepted by the Rabbinical Schools, not noticing how little value our Lord Himself set upon their traditions, and not considering that from their wholly uncritical and dogmatic habits of mind the rulers of the Jewish Church were much less capable than we are of determining questions of authorship and date. We must then at the outset refuse to be guided by the judgment of the Jews themselves in forming our opinions about the Law; we must always try to approach the subject as free as possible from the prejudices which their dogmatism has created. And indeed it must be considered a very singular fact that we most of us implicitly believe, and even passionately defend, their unfounded and unscholarly assertions about the literary composition of their books, while we as unhesitatingly reject, what they were much more capable of forming an opinion upon, their interpretation of the books.

It follows that we can by no means hold it decisive of the authorship of the Pentateuch that the Synagogue uniformly ascribed it to Moses; the same school of thought which ascribed the Pentateuch to Moses was unable to recognize our

Lord as the Messiah, and was castigated by His stern judgments in the most unsparing way.

But, as an additional encouragement to a calm and unprejudiced inquiry into the origin and the authorship of the Pentateuch, we may always remember this: its spiritual value for us cannot be affected by the results of the inquiry. The Pentateuch does not contain our rule of conduct or articles of belief; its moral teaching, no less than its ceremonial Law, has for us received its fulfilment in Christ, and to Christ we go, not to it. Its interest for us is that it was the Law of the Jewish Church in the time of our Lord, the full code, liturgy, and rubric of the people among whom He appeared. What attracts us in its study is that we can trace throughout how He realized all its typology and satisfied all its aspirations, going always to the Divine root of the matter, eliciting the spirit of it, and thereby often shattering its letter. Now supposing the book had been compiled actually by His contemporaries, this practical value of it would remain just what it is. For Jews, of course, who attempt to live by it still, it is of vast importance to establish its Mosaic origin, and so to play it off, as it were, against the authority of the Lord. For us the one important point is that the authority of the Lord is supreme over it, and that while He takes His stand upon it our eyes are turned not to it but to Him. It is of the utmost importance to bear in mind that when we speak of the Pentateuch as inspired, we do not mean and cannot mean what the Jew means, that it is our authority in conduct and in worship. We could not attempt, we do not wish to attempt, to practise the precepts of the Law which St. Paul denounced with all the vehemence of his spirit, showing that "Christ is the end of the Law to every one that believeth." When we speak of the Inspiration of the Pentateuch, we can only mean that it played a part in the economy of God's education of the human race, and therefore must always occupy a place in the Sacred Volume which is the sum of the revelation of God to man. And when we want to define more in detail what is to be included under this idea of Inspiration, there is one method, and one method only, open to us: we have to patiently study the book, find out all that is verifiable concerning it, and then making ample allowance for all the facts which are established, to say, 'Such and such is the Inspired Book of the Law.' To approach the subject with an *à priori* theory is fatal: to say, for instance, that the Inspired Law must all have come from Moses, or even from any single author, or any single age; to say that every statement in the volume, historical or scientific, is guaranteed by the Holy Spirit; or indeed to say anything about it which the clear facts of its contents or composition are liable to overthrow, is not to serve God nor yet to strengthen the authority of Scripture; it is to fly in the face of Truth, to deliver oneself over to a lie, and so to commit, as far as we are able, an unpardonable sin against the Spirit of God.

Now we will suppose ourselves living in the generation just before our Lord came to the earth, living in Judæa among the Scribes or Guardians of the Law: for three hundred years at least—as long, let us say, as the English Prayer Book has occupied a similar position in the English Church—the Law has been accepted almost exactly in its existing form, and guarded with scrupulous care by generation after generation of Scribes, as the Inspired and authoritative Rule for the Jewish Church. We inquire, When was this written, and who wrote it? "It was written," is the answer, "by Moses nearly 1500 years ago." "But how is this?" we inquire: "it contains an account of the death of Moses, speaks about no one knowing his sepulchre ' unto this day,' and even says 'there arose not a prophet since in Israel like unto Moses.' Are we to believe that he said this of himself?" "Yes," answer our teachers; "he was enabled to give this account of his own death prophetically."[1] But supposing we have carried back into that day the spirit of modern inquiry, we ask, "What authority is there for this? Does the book say that Moses wrote it? Does he speak throughout in his own person?" "No, certainly not," is the answer; "but the traditions of the Elders for these last three hundred years assure us unquestioningly that Moses is the author!"

[1] This is maintained by Josephus and Philo : the Talmud, on the other hand, says that Deut. xxxiv. was added by Joshua.

"Then how about the previous eleven or twelve hundred years?" There is silence.

All we can say, then, is that among the Jews returned from the Captivity, in the third century B.C., about 1200 years after Moses, the book was held as coming from the pen of the great founder of the national life and religion.

Our suspicions, we will suppose, are aroused. We say, Have these Rabbis then been imposing upon us, expecting us to accept their assertion without a particle of evidence? and we are driven to examine the book itself to see whether it could have been written by Moses. A brief examination shows that a good deal of it might have been written by him, but on the other hand a good deal could not have been written by him, except on the Rabbinical supposition that he wrote in a prophetic ecstasy which enabled him to describe future things in the past tense.

Let us look at two or three of the passages which could not have been written by Moses. In the book which we call Genesis, we once or twice read, "the Canaanite was then in the land" (Gen. xii. 6, xiii. 7). At the time when Moses lived, when the land was as yet in undisputed possession of the Canaanite, the remark would have been quite pointless; it could only have come from a writer who was looking back to the time before the Israelite conquest and possession of the land. Again, in Genesis xiv. 14 we read that Abram pursued the kings "as far as Dan"; but when

Moses wrote there was no place of that name; it was only afterwards, in the time of the Judges, that the Danites called the city of Laish after the name of their father Dan (Judges xviii. 29). Now, to take an instance from the second book, we read in Exod. xvi. 35 how "the children of Israel did eat the manna forty years until they came to a land inhabited." Of course this might have been said just in the last few months of Moses' life; but it would require us to suppose that he wrote the book quite at the end of forty years, and certainly would sound much more natural coming from a later writer looking back upon the past. To look at the third book, there is a passage (Levit. xviii. 25) which speaks of the land as "vomiting out the nations which were before you," in a way that implies that the expulsion is already effected. If this is the meaning of the words, then of course we should perceive that it is not Moses who is speaking, since at his death the nations of the land were still unassailed. In the fourth of our books we have a paragraph which begins, "while the children of Israel were in the wilderness" (Numb. xv. 32), which seems as if the writer were looking back on that time, and not speaking of what was still the condition of things. In the fifth book, too, we meet with many expressions which we certainly should not have put down to Moses unless the Rabbis had assured us of his authorship. Thus in ii. 12 we read that the Edomites drove out the Horites "as

Israel did unto the land of his possession," which must have been written by one who could look upon Israel's occupation of the land as an accomplished fact, which Moses of course could not have done. Look again at iii. 8, and you find, as in other places of the Pentateuch, the eastward countries described as "beyond Jordan," a description which could only be used by a writer in Palestine, west of Jordan. Moses, we know, never crossed the Jordan ; for him therefore Palestine itself, and not the land of the Amorites, would have been "beyond Jordan."[1] And the statements of the eleventh verse would certainly come very strangely from Moses. The writer speaks of the victory over Og as though it lay in a somewhat distant past, and a kind of legendary interest attaches to his bedstead which is kept at Rabbah ; but the war with Og was one of the later achievements of Moses' life (*vid.* Numb. xxi. 33). Again, in the fourteenth verse we read that Bashan was called Havvoth-jair, after Jair the son of Manasseh ; but, if we are to credit Judges x. 3, the name was derived from Jair the Judge three hundred years later ; while the addition of the words "unto this day" shows us that Moses is not the writer.

Perhaps we may give one further instance because it is peculiarly interesting. In one place a quotation is given from a work which is called the "Book of the wars of the Lord" (Numb. xxi. 14). It would be more natural to suppose that the

---

[1] Cf. Deut. i. 1, 5, with iii. 20, 25, xi. 30.

"wars of the Lord" were the wars which Jehovah's people waged against their neighbours when they were established in the Land; they might have been, of course, the wars of the conquest of the Land; but when Moses wrote, such a book could hardly have existed, or if it had been recently written in the camp to celebrate the victories just obtained over Og and Sihon, he would not have quoted it to establish a geographical point in the country where he was writing; he himself would have been quite as valuable an authority.

The closing chapters, again, of the Pentateuch speak of Moses as living long ago, and form an estimate of his historical position just as the Book of Numbers speaks of the great leader as "one who was very meek above all men on the face of the earth" (Numb. xii. 3), which could certainly have never come from the pen of Moses himself, for to speak about one's own meekness is dangerously near to forfeiting one's claim to the virtue.

From these instances alone we should have to conclude that the Pentateuch was not written by Moses; there may of course be a great deal of it from his pen; whole sections may have been preserved intact, but the actual writer from whom we receive the book must be one who wrote long after Moses was dead.

But now as we are driven to examine the books a little more carefully, we find that so far from being written by Moses, they are really of a very composite character, containing many enactments which must belong to different dates, because they are not reconcilable with one another, and many narratives, which are compiled from pre-existing narratives and which attempt with more or less success to work the different traditions into a unified whole. And in fact many of the phenomena throughout the work would be quite inexplicable except on the supposition that an editor was dealing with documents of a bygone age, and labouring under the disadvantage of being far removed from the events of which he writes. The full force of this remark could only be brought out by a very lengthy examination of all the books; but the general justice of it may be shown by a few examples.

Let us begin with a very decisive one. Turn to the twentieth chapter of Numbers. In the first verse we read how the people came to Kadesh "in the first month." As the last date mentioned was in the second year after the exodus (ch. x. 11), we must suppose that the "first month" is the first month of the third year, though the year is not actually mentioned. At verse twenty-two the narrative describes the journey from Kadesh to Mount Hor, and the death of Aaron on the mountain. But this has suddenly carried us over thirty-eight years, for, as we are expressly told (ch. xxxiii. 38), Aaron died in "the fortieth year after the children of Israel were come up out of the land of Egypt." This perfectly unmarked transition from the early encampment at Kadesh to the last year of the wandering could not be explained if Moses were writing; he of course would be perfectly clear on such a point: but it is at once explained if we recognize a later writer combining ancient documents in a single narrative and not clearly distinguishing the different dates. This single instance would at once convince us, but for the prejudice with which we generally start, that the book as we have it is not from the pen of Moses.

Next we may examine some of the legal enactments which point to different strata of legislation, and could not very intelligibly come from one legislator ; or if they did, would have been clearly distinguished as superseding or supplementing one another.

In the Book of Exodus (xxiii. 14) three feasts unto the Lord are ordained—the Feast of Unleavened Bread, which came in the spring when the young barley was just ripening, the Feast of Harvest, and the Feast of Ingathering. In Deuteronomy, again, the three feasts are enjoined, and more ample details are given, special names being applied to them—the Passover, the Feast of Weeks, and the Feast of Tabernacles (Deut. xvi.). These two accounts are quite consistent with one another, though the one in Deuteronomy has the appearance of being a later development, an adaptation of agricultural festivals to a growing precision of ceremonial observance. But in the intermediate books of Leviticus and Numbers there are directions given for the " set feasts of the Lord " which are of a far more elaborate character. We must turn to Lev. xxiii. and to Numbers xxviii., and read carefully through all the details. We find the first feast marked off into two parts, the Lord's Passover and the Feast of Unleavened Bread; the second feast is now carefully defined to take place seven times seven days after the first sheaf is garnered, whence it received in Hellenistic days the name Pentecost; then the third feast is divided into three, and the seventh month becomes almost wholly occupied with the observances, the Blowing of Trumpets at the beginning, the Day of Atonement on the tenth, the Feast of Tabernacles on the fifteenth. All this is very intelligible if we have the later growth incorporated in the books of Numbers and Leviticus, but hardly intelligible if we have to suppose that Moses composed the whole code of legislation. For we might well ask, Why did he not in one simple passage give all at once? What need of a fourfold repetition of the ordinance of the national feasts? It is indeed a kind of slur upon the wisdom of the legislator to suppose that he would have taught his people in that confusing way.

Let us take another illustration. In the wonderful chapter (Exod. xx.) which contains the Ten Words, as they are called, directions are given for making an altar of earth for the burnt offerings, and it is added, "in every place where I record my name I will come unto thee, and I will bless thee;" and in the glimpses we get into the early history of Israel, for instance in the deeds of the great prophet Samuel, the practice referred to in these directions is quite recognized as of Divine authority: in many places as occasion serves an altar is made and sacrifices are offered to the Lord. But in very striking contrast with this ordinance and the practice which it recognizes, the Book of Deuteronomy is constantly insisting that there shall only be one altar and one sanctuary. Look, for instance, at the twelfth chapter, and especially at the fifth verse; what is said there is the keynote of all the laws and arrangements of this book. Now if we are not to recognize here two strata of legislation, the first dating from very early times, the second representing a much later conviction of the need of centralizing and unifying the worship of Jehovah, we are placed certainly in a very difficult position for understanding the enactments. If we were to insist that both principles—the principle of many sacred places, and the principle of one sacred place only—were promulgated by Moses in one book proceeding from his sole pen, without any attempt to show how the one affected the other, we might be standing up for our preconceived notion of what an Inspired Pentateuch should mean, but we should certainly be seriously injuring the notion we ought to entertain about the dealings of God with men. Happily we are not called upon to maintain that Moses wrote these two passages, and therefore we are at liberty to recognize that they represent different stages in the development of the national cultus.

Another instance of a similar kind will bring into clearer relief the difficulties in which we should be landed if we had to maintain that Moses wrote the Pentateuch as it stands. In the Book of Deuteronomy we may observe that there is no distinction drawn between priests and Levites. The sacred duties are to be performed by "the priests, the sons of Levi," "the priests, the Levites" (see Deut. x. 8, 9, xviii. 1, xxi. 5). But in those parts of the Pentateuch which, as we saw in the case of the Feasts, represent a later development of ceremonial practice, especially in Leviticus and Numbers, there is a very sharp distinction drawn between the priests, "the sons of Aaron," and the far inferior body of the Levites. The familiar story of Korah illustrates this fact. In the Book of Deuteronomy (xi. 6) Korah is not mentioned in connection with Dathan's and Abiram's rebellion against the authority of Moses; but in the Book of Numbers (chap. xvi.) Korah is introduced, and his insurrection against the authority of the priests is interwoven with the narrative. Indeed, as the chapter stands it would seem that the great sin of the rebellion which was punished by the earth opening and swallowing the rebels, was that Korah, being a Levite only, aspired to do the work of a priest. The moral of the episode is pointed thus ; it was "to be a memorial unto the children of Israel, to the end that no stranger which is not of the seed of Aaron come near to burn incense before the Lord" (ver. 40). The only explanation of this would be that at one time the whole body of the Levites were recognized as the priests of Jehovah, and then afterwards a special family was recognized as the priestly family. But if this is the conclusion to which the facts point, it is quite certain that one and the same author would not introduce the two stages of development, exactly on the same historical plane.

This general view of the relation of these two strata receives additional confirmation in proportion to the attention with which the books are studied. Two facts may be briefly mentioned here. In the legislation of Deuteronomy great stress is laid upon this, that the Levites, as a tribe, should be without a portion in the distribution of the land; the Lord was to be Levi's portion. The second fact arising out of this portionless position of the Levite is that, throughout the book of Deuteronomy, he is always numbered with " the widow and the orphan and the stranger within the gates" (Deut. xii. 19, xiv. 27, xvi. 11. xviii. 6, xxvi. 11); accordingly when the tithes are brought up to the Lord's house, to be eaten in the presence of the Lord, with joy and thanksgiving, the Levites, along with the other unpropertied classes, are to be invited to the feast—" thou shalt not forsake him, the Levite, for he hath no portion nor inheritance with thee" (Deut. xiv. 27, xxvi. 12-15).

All this breathes the spirit of a very simple and primitive faith. Feasting is a sacrifice to

Jehovah; and Jehovah's peculiar servants depending entirely upon the gifts of the people are called to be partakers of the good cheer to which they cannot contribute.

In the books of Leviticus and Numbers a very different aspect is put upon the institution of the priesthood and the tithes. In the 35th chapter of Numbers orders are given to set apart certain cities for the Levites. So far from being "without portion and inheritance," they are to have forty-eight cities of their own with considerable suburbs; as each city is to have a territory of nearly a square mile, for the cattle and substance and beasts of the Levites, it is clear that the priestly order is here supposed to be tolerably well off; and not only is this land to be apportioned to them, it is expressly enacted that they should hold it as an inalienable possession, which may not even be sold (Lev. xxv. 34). Accordingly, in the division of the land under Joshua these dispositions are immediately made (Josh. xxi.). In agreement with this changed position of the Levites is the ordinance for the tithes which is given in Leviticus xxvii. 32 and Numbers xviii. 21-32. In place of the people assembling to feast, and inviting the Levites, as poor and portionless brethren, the people are not allowed to come to the Sanctuary themselves (Numb. xviii. 22), but they are to hand their tithes over to the Levites, and the Levites are to give a tithe of these tithes to the priests.

It would be quite out of the question to suppose

that Moses, writing the three treatises, Leviticus, Numbers, and Deuteronomy, would in the two first make arrangements for giving to the Levites cities and territory, and in the last uniformly treat them as quite portionless. This would be to charge the inspired legislator with a most egregious inconsistency. It is only the curious blindness induced by a dogmatic pre-supposition that can account for this singular oversight: it has been thought that we were vindicating the Divine inspiration of Moses by maintaining that he could have given these totally inconsistent laws. The difficulty of course immediately melts away when we recognize that in Leviticus and Numbers are incorporated much later regulations which were applicable in a more advanced stage of the hierarchical development.

Directly these different strata in the Pentateuch are recognized, many small points which are exceedingly puzzling while we are treating the whole as the work of one author, become quite plain We may look for one moment at two such elucidations. In the fourth chapter of Numbers the age of the active Levites is specified; they are to be "from thirty years old and upward even unto fifty years old." In the eight chapter of the same book (ver. 24) the age is lowered to twenty-five. As a correction, representing quite another period when reason had arisen for accepting the service of younger men, this is plain and simple enough. As a regulation coming from the same legislator who made the regulation of chapter iv., in the same breath as it were, it would be unintelligible indeed.

And so in the old Book of the Covenant, as Exodus xx. 23–xxiii. 33 is called, there is a regulation made for slave-holding in Israel. A man might buy his brother as a slave, but only for six years' service; at the beginning of the seventh year the slave would be free, and might go out with his wife. In Deuteronomy (xv. 12–18) the same law is repeated, with a further injunction that the slave owner in dismissing his freedman should make him a substantial present from the flock, the threshing-floor, and the winepress. This law of slavery, when contrasted with the practice of antiquity generally, cannot be called severe; on the contrary it is remarkably considerate and humane. But in the statutes of Leviticus even this is considerably modified: an Israelite is not to make his brother serve as a bondservant at all, but as a hired servant (Levit. xxv. 39). On the other hand this mitigated form of bondage is not to terminate with six years' service, but only at the Jubilee, which might be one or might be forty-nine years off (ver. 40). It is quite evident that these two divergent regulations would not stand side by side in the work of one legislator, unless some indication were given that the one was a correction of the other. In the present instance one regulation is given in Exodus, another in Leviticus, and then the first is repeated in Deuteronomy. Is it, in the face of a fact like this, honouring either God or Moses to maintain that Moses wrote the Pentateuch as it stands?

After what has been said it will be enough simply to refer to the frequent repetitions of laws even in successive sections of the Pentateuch, such repetitions as no one author would feel it necessary to make. When the repetition is an exact reproduction or when it is a remarkable variation, in either case the supposition of a common author is hard to maintain. Read through Leviticus xx., and you will find that through the greater part it is repeating chapter xviii. Or look at Exodus xxxiv. 14-26, and you will find Ten Commandments which are to be written down as a covenant between the Lord and His people; from the beginning of the chapter it would almost seem as if these were the original commandments written on the tables of stone. But in chapter xx. there is another and more compact version of the Ten Words, which is distinguished from the version in chapter xxxiv. by a much stronger insistance upon the ethical side of the code.

But it is time to ask, How in the face of all these very obvious facts, facts which require no erudition to discover but lie on the surface of the book itself, how comes it that Moses was reputed as the author? and how are we to explain the phenomena of the different strata which we seem to detect in the Pentateuch? To the answer of these two questions we must now address ourselves.

And first, Why has Moses been so generally credited with the authorship, when almost the immediate result of a careful inquiry is to show that he could not have written the Pentateuch as it lies before us? Well, it is very certain that Moses the great leader of the Exodus was universally believed to have written a "Law;" how large it was we cannot tell, but presumably it was comparatively brief, for in the Book of Joshua (viii. 32) we are told that it could all be written upon the stones of a single altar. In Exodus (xxxiv. 27) a commandment is given to Moses to write the law that has just been promulgated. In the twenty-fourth chapter this Book of the Covenant is referred to as a definite work (vers. 4-7) which by the very fact of its being mentioned in Exodus is shown not to have been the Pentateuch of which Exodus is a part.

There are some other allusions in the book to writings of Moses. Thus he is told to write the account of the war with Amalek in a book (Exod. xvii. 14). And again he wrote a record of the journeys of the children of Israel (Numb. xxxiii.). We may observe here that the quite modern deciphering of all the buried literature of Egypt, and the discovery of works which date from a period long before Moses, has shown how absurd it would be to deny on *à priori* grounds that Moses could have written a Law-book. That Moses might have written a work which covers the ground of the Pentateuch is beyond question. The only question is whether we have reason to suppose that he actually did. Now from the facts just quoted it seems highly probable that Moses did write a Law-book and a historical memorial of the events in which he played the leading part ; and it seems likely enough, though it cannot be demonstrated, that in Exodus xx. 23–xxiii. 33 we have an extract from that law-book, if not a copy of it, and that in Exodus xxxiv. 10–26 we have another writing of Moses, and that Numbers xxxiii. is drawn from his itinerarium. This is all possible, but it is to be clearly noticed that the books never lay claim in any part to be written by Moses, and therefore we have no right to lay stress on his authorship even in the case of these fragments.

Granted, however, that ancient writings of Moses were current from the earliest times, it would be quite in accordance with all that we know of literary practices in antiquity, that as the Law grew round the nucleus of the Mosaic Law (Torah), and as the narrative was collected and mounted to form the framework of the Law, the ever-enlarging book so produced should be always referred to as the Book of Moses. We must remember that the book would not be published and circulated in the modern sense of the terms ; it would remain in the hands of the prophets or priests who taught the people. As bit by bit was added to the Institutes there would be no attempt to distinguish the new from the old, and the law-book, whenever it was referred to, would always be regarded as the law-book of the great legislator.

The more we try to conceive the actual facts of the primitive history, the more intelligible it will appear that tradition should ascribe the writing of the Pentateuch to Moses, and the more impossible it will appear to admit that tradition was right.

But now we are forced to seek an answer for our second question. Here we have a Book of Laws stereotyped and accepted from about the third century B.C.; and on investigation we have seen that it betrays evidence of several different strata of legislation. Incidentally the illustrations we took exhibited three stages of development. There was the stage of very primitive and simple practice, when many altars were recognized as sanctuaries of worship, and when the three festivals of the year were closely connected with the Seasons. Then there was a stage in which the many altars became One, and the One Sanctuary being supreme, the local sanctuaries with their many idolatrous tendencies were condemned and gradually abolished. At this stage the priestly office appears in the hands of a Levitical tribe which has no material status in the country, but depends upon the tithe offerings of the people. Finally, there is a stage at which the whole position of Sanctuary and Priesthood is much more defined.; the Priests are separated from their inferior ministers, the Levites, while all the sacred tribe has a recognized status, with cities and lands of its own, and the tithes are given to it as a tribute. At this stage the three primitive festivals have undergone a remarkable expansion and a minute definition.

How is all this to be explained? Well, it becomes intelligible if we take firm hold of the idea of a Sacred Law which grew with the national life. Suppose for the sake of clearness that to Moses in the first instance was revealed the complete ideal scheme of Temple, Hierarchy, and Cultus as it finally existed after the Captivity. It was not carried out at first. This is plain, not only from the Book of Judges and the early histories, but also from the writings of the prophets. What was actually carried out was the primitive application of the Divine Law, which is to be observed in the first stage that we have just been looking at. Books were written containing the injunctions ; narratives were written which exhibited these injunctions in practice, or in struggling conflict with elements of heathenism all around, narratives such as are preserved for us in primitive vigour by the Book of Judges.

Slowly was the Divine purpose fulfilled : during the time of the kings, Jehovah's prophets were laboriously leading the people to a greater purity of worship ; books were written which exhibited the Ancient Law in the form in which it appears in Deuteronomy. Thus another step was taken in the realization of the ideal which we have supposed was presented to Moses : the Sanctuary at Jerusalem became the acknowledged centre of Israel's religious life. Still slowly through national disaster, the captivity and its sufferings, prophets strove to point the lessons of the Divine teaching. Books were written which exhibited the Ancient Law in the form which is presented by the prophet Ezekiel. With the exception possibly of the High Priest and the Day of Atonement, Ezekiel recognizes the Law in its full development. Then came the great period of national restoration in the fifth century B.C. Ezra and his fellow-workers had as their life task to bring the Ancient Law into accordance with the new developments of Divine truth. The law-books and associated narratives which had appeared at the different stages of growth had all to be incorporated in one single work. The ideal which on our supposition was revealed to Moses, now began to fill in and complete itself. For instance, we are told how now for the first time the Feast of Tabernacles was genuinely kept (Nehem. viii. 17).

The Pentateuch, then, as we have it, would represent the Ancient Mosaic Law as it was finally shaped after the return of the Jews from Babylon to the Holy Land. Like an organic growth, as it certainly is, it retains in its very form the elements which it assimilated. It enables us even now, if we bestow some patience upon it, to detect underneath the completed Work the previous works belonging to earlier times which it has taken into itself. Thus it is a single unified whole, but it is as far as possible from being a mechanical unity such as would result from a single author composing it as a single work.

Before we sum up the chapter and pass away from the subject, we ought perhaps to notice how this composite character which comes from the method of growth is exhibited in many of the narratives, and especially in that wonderful and inestimable book which we call by its Greek name Genesis, but which the Jew calls " In the beginning." Even a careless reader of Genesis will often notice how the narrative consists of two or more versions of the same event blended together. A now very familiar example is to be found in the first two chapters. From chapter i. to the end of the third verse of chapter ii. is a connected account of the Creation, which proceeds from the making of light on the first day to the making of man on the sixth, and then follows the Sabbath. But at verse four of chapter ii., another narrative begins; according to this narrative man is made first, then comes the springing of the herbs ; then woman is made, and finally the animals are formed out of the ground. The second narrative seems much the more primitive, and the first may probably be traced to a far advanced view of God which was the result of ages of faith in Him.[1]

[1] These two versions of the Creation are marked by a striking difference in the name which is used for God. In the second He is called by the name which is rendered in our Bibles Jehovah ; in the first He is called Elohim, which is another form of El, the simplest title for God. It is worth while to notice this, because it was by this very obvious difference of usage that scholars were first started upon the task of distinguishing the different strata of the Pentateuch.

Or, again, look at chapter iv. 16–24, which gives us a very ancient account of Cain, tracing the family tree through Enoch and Methushael, to Lamech. But in chapter v. quite another start is made, and Lamech's family is traced up to Adam through Methuselah, Enoch, and Seth. Or study the account of the flood, and you will find that it is a very careful combination of two narratives, one of which only stated that the animals went into the ark by pairs, while the other said that the clean beasts were taken in by sevens. If the reader will take a little pains, he will observe that the two narratives can be untwisted still. Starting from Genesis vi. 13, he will find that he may eliminate the following passages, vii. 1–5, 7, 8, 10, 12, 16, 17, 22, 23 ; viii. 2 (last clause), 3, 6–12, 20–22, and these eliminated passages will form a separate and consistent narrative, while the rest forms the later narrative which was incorporated with it.

Let us look only at one other brief instance of two narratives admitted into the text, though in this case there is no attempt at combination. We have two irreconcileable accounts of Esau's wives. Look at chapters xxvi. 34 and xxviii. 9 ; then look at xxxvi. 2. You will see that the traditions were by no means consistent ; put them side by side, thus :—

1. Judith, daughter of Beeri, the Hittite.	1. Oholibamah, daughter of Anah.
2. Basemath, daughter of Elon, the Hittite.	2. Adah, daughter of Elon, the Hittite.

| 3. Mahalath, daughter of Ishmael, sister of Nebaioth. | 3. Basemath, daughter of Ishmael, sister of Nebaioth. |

But we must bring this chapter to a close. There are some of us to whom it will present quite a new conception of the Pentateuch; but there are none of us who ought to feel that our conception has been lowered by examination of these facts. If we are disposed to say at the end of our investigation, "We do not call a book which has such an origin inspired at all," then we ought to see how mistaken our idea of inspiration has been. Inspired the book is; and considering the place it holds in the history of revelation and especially in the chain of facts which ended in the coming of our Lord, we shall not readily allow any arguments of criticism to affect our conviction of its inspiration; but we may well accept, and joyfully welcome, the work of criticism which has been throwing such wonderful and unexpected lights on the slow growth, the organic expansion, by which our inspired Pentateuch, or Hexateuch, reached its present form. It might be urged that since the Law was for Christians superseded by Christ, the whole study of the Pentateuch is of merely an antiquarian interest; but indeed if the explanation of the phenomena it presents, which we have just been considering, should prove to be correct and should meet with general acceptance, this antiquarian interest would pass into an interest of a much more living kind; for we should have here a most striking example of the way in which God gradually unfolds Himself to the world, and likewise an example of the way in which our own prejudices and misdirected zeal often hinder us for generations from understanding His unfolding. A certain loss in the naïve simplicity with which we have usually contemplated the book will be abundantly compensated by a deeper understanding of the Divine plan which is working itself out in the world.

CHAPTER VIII.

THE POETRY AND THE MISCELLANEOUS WRITINGS OF THE INSPIRED BOOK.

BESIDES the Prophets, and the Histories and the Law, there is in the Old Testament a little group of books which in our Bible is inserted between the Histories and the Prophets, but in the Hebrew Bible finds a place after the Prophets. This group in the time of our Lord was called by a Greek name which signifies Holy Scriptures,[1] and was treated as subordinate to the two great groups of the Law and the Prophets in authority and general value. These six books are, according to the general admission, inspired; but even the most uncritical reader is conscious of immense differences between them, and no less differences between their several parts. In the popular use

---

[1] The Hagiographa in the Hebrew Canon included some books which we have examined under the Histories, and some to which we have not yet referred. The Chronicles, Ezra, and Nehemiah, as much later in origin than the Kings, were placed in this inferior list. The books of Ruth and Esther had a place here too.

of the word inspiration, one would be inclined to say there is less inspiration in the Book of Esther than in the Book of Job, less inspiration in the Book of Ecclesiastes than in the Book of Proverbs, less inspiration in the Song of Songs than in the Psalter. But our inquiries hitherto must have made us very doubtful whether this popular use of the word inspiration is very serviceable, and whether indeed it is not somewhat misleading. If we are to go on the lines which have been gradually clearing before our eyes in previous chapters, we shall state the truth contained in the judgment just passed in a slightly different way. We shall say that in our Inspired Bible there are writings which owe their canonical position to very various causes, and that therefore the same rule of interpretation and treatment cannot apply to them all. Starting from the recognition of the canonical collection, allowing the right of all these works to occupy their places in the Inspired Writings, we have to exercise all our faculties to discover what is to be discovered about the general setting, if we may so express it, of each particular book; we have to inquire, Who wrote it? or if that is a fruitless inquiry, When was it written? or failing this, or in addition to this, we have to consider what was the occasion of its production, and what was the scope of its purpose? The result of these inquiries will often be to greatly modify existing opinions, and, let us add, to clear away many difficulties which perplex the unthinking believer as well as the thinking unbeliever. For instance, the result of such inquiry may be to show that a book or part of a book had its origin in a set of circumstances which has now passed away, and therefore its teaching is not of direct application. In such a case, the presence of the book in our Bible is not to imply that its precepts are to form our rule of conduct, or its delineations of character to form the models for our imitation. The work may occupy its place in the Inspired Book for quite another reason; and therefore to allow that by its inspiration is meant that it is an authoritative statement of eternal truth and a code of law for our Christian life, may prove to be unchristian and harmful in the highest degree. Let us take an instance which is very familiar, and we may add, often very puzzling. Very frequently in the Psalms we are startled by fierce and vindictive utterances such as these: "Be not merciful to any wicked transgressors" (lix. 5). "Break their teeth," says the fifty-eighth psalm, in speaking of the wicked, "let them melt away as water, &c."; and then it adds, "the righteous shall rejoice when he seeth the vengeance." This is an example of what constantly occurs throughout. What are we to make of it? Is this the temper in which we are to regard the wicked? Are we to hate them with a perfect hatred? Are we to rejoice at the punishment which falls upon them? Clearly we are not; to treat these expressions as the utterance of the

Divine Wisdom would be to deny Christ; and in some cases where men have breathed the spirit of these imprecatory passages, they have in the name of God brought shame upon the name of the Saviour. We are here in some danger: we may easily allow a theory of inspiration to form in our minds which would make these outbursts of elemental passion the expression of the Spirit of God. We are bound, therefore, to determine with the utmost care what attitude these psalms assume, how they stand in reference to our moral and spiritual ideas.

Again, in some of the writings now before us a mournful pessimism is expressed, which arises from a limitation of outlook, from a belief that "there is no work, nor device, nor knowledge, nor wisdom in the grave whither" we go (Eccl. ix. 10). "The dead," says the Psalmist (Ps. cxv. 17), "praise not the Lord, neither any that go down into silence;" and, "In death there is no remembrance of thee: in Sheol who shall give thee thanks?" (Ps. vi. 5). "Wilt thou show wonders to the dead? Shall they that are deceased arise and praise thee?" (Ps. lxxxviii. 10). Sometimes we think that we are honouring God by speaking of all the utterances of the Bible as if they came from His lips, and were literally His words: now what a terrible teaching it is that the God who, according to our Lord's teaching, had shown wonders to the dead, raising up Abraham, for instance, to live with Him for ever, has uttered these sentences as the word of His truth. From that ill-considered phrase, "the Word of God," as applied to the Inspired Book, has arisen mischief incalculable. "This is the word of God, you tell me," says the perplexed youth who is beginning to read and to think; "these statements, then, concerning the silence and extinction of the dead are His words; He, therefore, teaches me not to believe in immortality." What a conclusion for us to lead a fellow-creature to by our ignorant and thoughtless dogmatism. The truth is, many utterances have a place in the Inspired Book just *because they are not* the word of God, but only the word of man—man's sorrowful questionings, doubtings, forebodings, blunderings, misunderstandings. In fact, one feature of the book which more than anything else secures it the place which it holds in human estimation, is that it accurately expresses all those half-dumb longings and vague imaginings which occupy the spirit of man, just because he is a man. Thus Jeremiah can exclaim, "O Lord, thou hast deceived me!" (Jer. xx. 7). As an inspired writer, is he here to be taken as stating a fact which God is virtually asserting through him? Surely not: he is uttering that grieved and agonized exclamation of human impatience which the servant of the Lord in his frailty often feels when, in obedience to the Lord's command, he has become a laughing-stock to the world.

One other instance will set the difficulty which arises in these books from a mechanical theory of inspiration in a singularly clear and intelligible light. In the last chapter of Proverbs we are told that kings and rulers should abstain from strong drink, in order that they may have all their faculties for their important duties; but at the same time a commandment is given to provide strong drink for the poor, the miserable, and the sorrowful, as well as for those who are in danger of dying (Prov. xxxi. 6, 7). The poor man is to drown the thought and memory of his poverty in this way. Now if this is the word of God, the people who are obeying Him in this particular are the proprietors of the public-houses in our crowded streets; and if our teachers insist on treating all the precepts of the Scriptures as the direct utterances of God for the guidance of our life, then the publican has as much right to quote this passage as the temperance lecturer has to quote that other passage, "Look not on the wine when it is red."

The danger to which we are exposed in these and similar instances can only be met by entirely dismissing all mechanical theories of inspiration, and patiently setting to work here, as in all the other books, to master the facts. In addition to the inquiries mentioned at the beginning of the chapter, we have always to put this further question: Having found who wrote this passage, when it was written, to whom it was written, am I to take the teaching as applicable to me and to Christians generally; or does it stand before me in the Bible possessed of a merely historical interest, showing me what once, in the slow unveiling of His full and perfect will, was applicable to, or believed by, the servants of God? Now perhaps a brief review of the six sacred writings with which we are now concerned may help to put us in the right attitude for understanding how they come to stand where they do, what meaning must be attached to their being inspired, and to what extent they are a code of ethical and spiritual precepts which have a Divine authority for *us*.

To begin with the Book of Esther. Its subject shows that it belongs to the period after the exile. It is a historical work written to preserve the origin of the Feast of Purim. We have to seek its value in this, that it throws a little light upon a point in the history of the Jewish people, and, as we have had occasion to see, the whole history of that people is 'inspired' because of the part it was called to play in God's revelation of Himself to mankind. When we have said this, we have said all that can be urged for the canonical value of the work. So far from claiming to be written by direct inspiration of God, the book never alludes to God at all; the whole story proceeds simply on the lines of ordinary historical narrative. We are at liberty to detect in the events a Divine Providence at work on behalf of the people in exile, but the book makes no reference to such an interpretation of the facts. On the other hand, we can by no means recognize any ethical value in the story as it is told. The simple and courageous patriotism of Esther is worthy of all admiration, and the fall of the wicked Haman is instructive; but the terrible spectacle of the Jews wreaking vengeance on the people in the midst of whom they lived, on account of a plot which had not been carried out and had only been conceived by the malignity of one man, is neither admirable nor instructive. This hideous outbreak of Semitic fanaticism, if it is to be treated as historically credible, can only be read by us with feelings of the strongest abhorrence, and if the writer tacitly gives his approbation to it, we have to be very careful in recognizing that the writer is in no sense that God whose teaching is expressed in the Sermon on the Mount. Our blood runs cold as we read (Esther ix. 5-17) how the fierce and pitiless exiles slew 500 men in Shushan the palace, and many more in the rest of the king's provinces! and how the beautiful Jewish queen, unsatiated with slaughter, asked for a further butchery, in which 300 more were slain in the palace, so that altogether 75,000 men perished; and how then the Jews "rested, and made it a day of feasting and gladness." To leave any room for supposing that God either approved the action or had it recorded for our admiration, is to confuse the moral sense, and to blaspheme the name of Him who has required us to love our enemies, supporting His law upon the great and wonderful fact that God Himself is love, and loves the world.

We all of us agree in condemning the Massacre

of St. Bartholomew, and should bitterly resent any plea that it was sanctioned by God in the interests of His truth; the same moral sense, itself the product of Christian faith, which leads us to condemn Catherine de Medici and Charles IX., must lead us to condemn even more strongly Esther the Queen and Mordecai the Jew, whose action as represented in this book is not determined by any religious conviction, but simply by a passionate vindictiveness. If the book has a moral for us at all, it is to be found in this, that Judaism, even in its ultimate development, was immeasurably distant from the Kingdom of God which Jesus came to found.

We now come to a very different book, the book of Job. This remarkable poem stands alone in the Hebrew literature. The author of it is unknown; but all the more striking must appear the religious consciousness of the people which could produce such an anonymous work. From the brief historical introduction and epilogue, it has been very hastily assumed that the whole poem is meant to be a statement of fact; and people holding a mechanical theory of inspiration are often scandalized by the discovery—the very first which a true Hebrew scholarship makes—that we are here dealing, not with a narrative of what actually happened, but with an ideal and poetical delineation under which the great problem of human suffering and sin is discussed. Few parts of the Scriptures afford us better illustrations of the incredible perversity to which human dogmatism on the subject of Inspiration has led us. Again and again texts are quoted from the speeches of Eliphaz, and Bildad, and Zophar, and even Elihu, as the "word of God." And yet the whole point of the book is that their speech, and indeed Job's own speech too, is one-sided and ignorant. When the Lord answers Job out of the whirlwind, He is represented as saying, "Who is this that darkeneth counsel by words without knowledge?" (xxxviii. 2). To quote the language of one who is described as darkening counsel by words without knowledge, and to maintain that it is the "word of God," is surely a very gratuitous blasphemy, a blasphemy against which the very book would protect us if we only read it with common attention. But no right judgment about the book can be formed unless its poetical character is recognized. Under the form of an episode, the scene of which is laid in remote patriarchal times, the poet presents the grave question, "Why is man born unto trouble? What do his afflictions mean? Are they the mark of God's anger, or the seal of his tender solicitude? And the answer is given—not quite decisively, but in a tentative way which is not altogether without its value even for us who have learnt to judge of suffering in the light of a Suffering Son of God. Trouble is not always the punishment of sin, but is sometimes a test and a proving which God sends to us through the Adversary; and the understanding of it is to be sought not in rash speculation, which can never find out God, but in the way of patient endurance. Yes, the spiritual lesson not only had its value at the time, it has a value for us, as St. James points out (James v. 11). But it is difficult for us not to lose all sense of its spiritual teaching in the wonder and delight which are produced by one of the most remarkable poems that ever came from human pen. It owes its place in the Canon doubtless to its spiritual teaching, but it keeps its place in our hearts by its unrivalled poetical beauty.

Now let us look at the Psalter. About no part of the Bible do we feel more confidence in asserting its inspiration. It is a spiritual fountain from which the human race has drawn living waters for generation after generation. In it men of many races, many ages, many ranks, have found refreshment and strength, guidance and instruction. At no time are we more sure that we are listening to a voice from beyond than when we are reading these psalms; from no part of the Scriptures do texts so frequently stand out as direct messages of comfort, or of exhortation. In the Psalms our own hearts seem to find their voice, to speak with God, and to receive His direct answers No aspect of the spiritual life, no passion of the human heart, no dark experience of desolation and despair, no bright enthusiasm of trust and hope, no sighing over the irreparable evil, no striving after the unattained good, no love, no hate, no doubt, no faith, no sorrow, no joy of the spirit of man, but finds expression here in language which is universal, because it is simple, elementary, true to experience. The position, then, of the Psalter is secured; no carping of objectors, no analysis of critics, can affect it. A clever man finds fault with the structure of Shakespere's plays; he finds that the dramatic unities have been set at naught, that anachronisms of the grossest kind have been admitted; that many passages are ungrammatical, others corrupt; that some passages are coarse and others commonplace. Well, he may urge his objections as ingeniously as he pleases: he will leave Shakespere just where he found him. Shakespere is Shakespere, be the critic who he may. His sovereignty does not rest on these things which the critic is discussing, but upon the abiding truth of his insight into the human heart; the human heart must recognize the truth so long as it is human. It is somewhat the same with the Psalter. We may well smile at criticism, if criticism thinks that it can assail the place which the Psalter holds. These psalms must always be read so long as the human race has to live in the shadowy mysteries of a world which it cannot comprehend, to walk the perilous path between the weary wastes of doubt and superstition, to listen for the voice of its Father and call to Him in the darkness.

It is this unassailable position of the Psalms which might give us serenity and confidence in making inquiries concerning their authorship and occasion, or concerning the collection of them into a single book. We might well have a very unprejudiced mind in considering whether they were composed by Israel's great king, David, by Israel's sorrowful poets in the land of their captivity, or by the heroic singers of Israel in the dark days of the Maccabees.

There was a time when a kind of vague impression prevailed that the Psalms were all written by David; and this, though the very titles of the larger part of them refer the composition to others. That David was the first psalm-singer in Israel was enough to make Psalm collectors call their collections by his name, in much the same way that the expansions of the Law from age to age were usually referred back to Moses. A certain number of psalms composed by the great king no doubt survived and appeared in the several collections; but it is perhaps now beyond the range of possibility to determine whether they have come down to us in the Psalter; and even if we may be sure that some are there, it is next to impossible to settle which they are. The titles which appear at the head of the psalms are only the guesses of scribes, though some of them are very ancient guesses. The value of these guesses may be estimated by one familiar example. The exquisite Psalm of Penitence (li.) was fitted by the Jewish editors to an event in the life of David, and yet, not to mention the marks of the later prophetic view of the sacrifices in the sixteenth verse (cf. Is. i. 11 ; Hos. vi. 6), the close of the psalm points to a time when the walls of Jerusalem were broken down, and not to a time when it was the royal city and in the height of its prosperity. Still more unfortunate is the attempt to fix the fifty-second psalm to the episode of Doeg. Imagine David breaking out into the exclamation of joy, " I will give thee thanks for ever because thou hast done it" (ver. 9), just when, through his fault, indeed through his deliberate lie (1 Sam. xxi. 2), the priests of Nob had just been slain by Doeg (1 Sam. xxii. 18). It is not necessary to give further examples; it is enough to get this insight into the way in which the editors attached psalms to David and tried to fit them into the circumstances of his life. We may safely say that if the value of the Psalms depended in the remotest degree upon a Davidic authorship, their value would disappear at the first touch of criticism ; but the fact is that in no single case is the value in the remotest degree affected by the question whether David or some other poet composed them.

Strictly speaking, the Psalter is what we should call a hymnal. It is a collection of a hundred and fifty hymns for use in private or in public worship. The hymns are taken from many periods. Supposing some are David's and some are Maccabean, the earliest must be separated from the latest by seven or eight hundred years. In this way we find an explanation of the difficulties which were noted at the beginning of this chapter: some of the hymns come from a time when there was no vivid belief in immortality, and Sheol was regarded as the gloomy abode of the shades of the departed. Others, again, come from a period when the shattering of the national hopes, the sorrows of the captivity, and the teaching of the prophets, had made a belief in immortality part of the accepted national creed. Apparent contradictions, then, in the religious spirit of the Psalms are not contradictions of the Spirit of God, but the differences of religious feeling and belief which are found in different stages of the spiritual life of man. Our Psalter is divided into five parts,[1] which are sometimes supposed to correspond to the five-fold division of the Law-book; but unfortunately the psalms are not arranged in the chronological order of their composition: if they were, we should be

[1] These five parts end respectively at Psalms xli., lxxii., lxxxix., cvi., and cl., and conclude each with a doxology. These books are liturgical, and each of them is arranged or collected on a distinct plan and has a distinctive character of its own. We may notice that the first division or book (Ps. i.-xli.) uses the name The Lord, Jehovah, or Jahve, almost exclusively; the second book uses the name God (or Elohim) for the Divine Being: and again, the last book or division has several psalms for use in temple pilgrimages, processions, or services (see especially Ps. cxxii.). These and many similar facts concerning the Psalter amply confirm the conclusion that the book is not so much a collection of one writer's or a few writers' verses, but the late systematized collection of poetical songs and verses for the temple use.

able to follow with an admiring eye the gradual
development of the nation's spiritual aspirations
and ethical ideas during the long centuries. In
default of this advantage, possessing in our book a
mixed collection of hymns drawn from all periods,
and set down together either from a fancied simi-
larity of subject or an accidental repitition of a
phrase, we are bound, if we would understand it,
to bear always in our mind the chronological question and to make allowance for it.

There is one matter connected with the Psalter
to which a brief allusion may be made. Some of
the psalms are regarded as Messianic (*e.g.* ii., viii.,
xvi., cx.: slightly apart from these, lxix., cxviii,:
and by rabbinical interpretation, xl., xli., xlv., lxviii.,
xcvii., cii.), that is to say they are thought to be
uttered by the prophetic Spirit, either as descriptions of Christ or as language actually appropriate
in the very lips of Christ. Every reader of the
New Testament, and especially the Acts of the
Apostles, is familiar with the arguments based
upon this belief. How is the belief affected by the
discovery that not David, nor yet any known
author, is the poet, but that these wonderful songs
come rather from the heart of the nation, are the
expression of the religious sentiment of the nation,
and therefore, like all the best songs, are remembered not because they came from a distinguished
pen, but because the obscure or anonymous author
succeeded in giving apt expression to the general
feeling?

We may glance for a moment at two of these Messianic Psalms—one which seems to express the victorious power and royal dignity of the coming Christ, another which seems to express His humiliation and suffering. The one is quite anonymous; the other is in the superscription ascribed to David. Let us look first at the second and then at the twenty-second psalm. The second psalm presents a perfect little intaglio. The Lord's anointed is seated on the holy hill of Zion—the kings of the earth are conspiring against him. High over Zion is the Lord Himself, the protector of His own anointed. The anointed king speaks, and his speech forms the central part of the poem. He utters his consciousness of the Lord's communion with Him; he recognizes the Lord as his Father, himself as begotten of God. Then the psalm closes with a forecast: this regal Son of God must conquer all the raging nations, and therefore the kings are urged to come and make their submission to him. David could not have said this of himself; no king of Israel could have said this of himself: but from David's time the nation was conscious of an ideal element in the kingship—a close relation between the king and Israel's one King, Jehovah, and a promise of world-wide empire which after David's reign always receded farther and farther from the range of historical possibility. Whenever a poet sang truly of this ideal element in the kingship, he was pointing forward to an event which he himself little understood: but when the fulness of time was come, the apostles of the Saviour recognized that in Him this ideal element descended into the region of reality (Acts iv. 25-28).

It would seem, then, that the Messianic character of the psalm would lose rather than gain by ascribing it to any particular author, or by supposing that it was written in any conscious power of forecasting the far off Divine event. The whole people of Israel was God's prophecy; the monarchy of Israel was a marked feature of that prophecy; the national, heroic, and patriotic songs which best uttered the self-consciousness of the people thus became the utterance of the prophecy; and in this way the best songs of the monarchy always point forward to Christ. An illustration may be allowed. The songs of the Scottish nation owe their power not to the personality of their authors, but to the representative character of their strains; they utter the tender pathos, the intense patriotism, the delight in mountain and flood, which mark the best Scotch natures; thus they moulded the national character in proportion as they sprang from it. In Israel pathos, patriotism, and local pride all took a peculiar form because of the peculiar destiny of the nation. Israel existed, and in its higher moments knew that it existed, in order to bring an untold blessing to all the nations; its pathos was in its sufferings for the salvation of the world, its patriotism was a passion for the Kingdom of God, its local pride in Mount Zion and in the hills and rivers of the Holy Land was only a thin disguise of the glorying in another "City which had foundations." It thus inevitably came about that the national poetry of Israel had what we should call a prophetic tinge throughout. In this sense all the psalms which refer to the national life are more or less Messianic, and the so-called Messianic Psalms only mark at its highest point a spiritual consciousness which was to be discovered throughout.

We are now in a position to understand Psalm xxii. This poem is ascribed to David, and some people point to the twenty-third chapter of the First Book of Samuel as furnishing an account of the circumstances in which it was composed. But clearly whether David wrote it or not is a matter of some indifference. It was the singular destiny of the chosen prophetic nation to achieve its work for the world through suffering and disaster. The monarchy which was the type of God's rule, was at once split into two, and through ever-dwindling splendour and importance passed to its final extinction in the Captivity. The people through whom deliverance was to come to the world must achieve its work through travail and sorrow: this fact is written in broad lines upon the history, and expressed with increasing clearness by successive prophetic writers. It naturally finds expression in the national poetry, and nowhere more beautifully and strikingly than in this particular psalm. This dark and sorrowful vein of feeling was completely understood when Christ, the King of Israel and the Priest of Israel, was offered upon the Cross as the Paschal Lamb. The Lord Himself in His sufferings could not fail to remark how He was bringing to fulfilment all that was found of this sort in the ancient scriptures, and in fact this special psalm came to His lips as He hung upon the cross. Yet, how cramping and distorting a view of the matter would it be to suppose that the author of the psalm was in any sense consciously forecasting the agony of Calvary: his point of view is quite different; he rejoices in his own humiliation because "the kingdom is the Lord's and He is the king among the nations;" he does not venture in any way to identify himself with that Supreme King, as Christ our Saviour does.

But it is time to leave the Book of the Psalms. As was said at the beginning, no attempts to define more exactly what is meant by their inspiration can in the least affect the certainty of that inspiration itself. About that point we may be always absolutely sure, and therefore we may the more freely shape our conceptions in such a way that we may not seem to attribute to the Spirit of God, or to seal with the mark of His approval, those expressions in the Psalter which exhibit but a low degree of spiritual faith or but a faint conception of a pure morality. To be perfectly definite, when we speak of the Psalmists as inspired, we cannot and do not mean that the passages which show an ignorance about the immortality of the soul, or the passages which breathe out cursings and threatenings against personal enemies, are in any sense whatever the words or the utterances of God. By inspiration we mean, as the facts show us, a much broader and less mechanical influence, which in the present instance may be best described as *the movements of the Divine Spirit in the national life and faith of Israel, which give to the representative utterances of its literature a certain prophetic and universal significance.* And from this idea we are able to explain the beautiful and familiar fact that in the Psalms almost all our religious desires and thoughts find a voice : the passion for holiness, the plea for pardon, the joy of forgiveness, the eagerness to proclaim what the soul has seen and tasted of the Lord, the assured serenity in face of the distressing problems of life, the exultation in presence of the visible universe which is as the garment of God, the terror of death, the triumph over it for ever. Certainly that would be an ill-taught and a straitened spirit which felt that there was any loss in surrendering a mechanical theory of Inspiration for the theory which the facts of the Psalm-book itself require us to hold.

We have now to look at three books in the Holy Writings, or Hagiographa, which have almost universally been ascribed to King Solomon ; and we may safely say that hundreds of persons have so confused the idea of authorship with that of inspiration, that they would feel a suspicion cast upon the authorship of Solomon to be a slur cast upon the inspiration of the books. Yet a moment's consideration will show what a confusion of thought this is. If we take the Book of Proverbs, for instance, we find that it falls into four sections. There is an introduction which comprises chapters one to nine. Then comes a collection of proverbs —which, it is needless to point out, the first nine chapters are not—this collection comprises chapters ten to twenty-four. Chapters twenty-five to twenty-nine form another collection of proverbs. Lastly, chapters thirty and thirty-one contain two 'prophecies,' the one a prophecy of a man named Agur, the other a prophecy which a King Lemuel received from his mother. This last section is clearly *not* written by Solomon. The second collection of proverbs was made by Hezekiah's scribes (*vid.* ch. xxv. 1); and though it is conceivable that the other sections of the book were written by Solomon, yet it is to be observed that no such claim is made by the book itself. The introduction to the Proverbs of Solomon, which occupies the first nine chapters, would seem rather to come from some one who was editing the famous king's sayings. Thus, all that the book itself says is that chapters x.–xxiv. 22, and chapters xxv.–xxix. are Solomon's utterances. It is to be noted that the last verses of chapter xxiv. are referred to some other wise man, and not to Solomon himself.

As to the Book of The Preacher, it would betray a most extraordinary ignorance of ancient literary ideas and methods to maintain that because the writer puts his composition into the lips of Solomon, he therefore wished it to pass as Solomon's own. It was a practice among the Jews, who had no laws of literary procedure corresponding to ours, to publish their thoughts under the name of a great man among the ancients. Thus the beautiful work called the Wisdom of Solomon which probably owes its exclusion from the Canon merely to its late origin and to the consequent fact that it was written in Greek and not in Hebrew, was in no sense of the word a forgery as we understand that term, because it passed current as the wisdom of the ancient king. There may be no reason for denying that The Preacher is King Solomon; but we must very carefully secure ourselves against the error that to question this is to dispute its inspiration. The same remark applies to the "Song of Songs," which contains in its superscription the title "which also is Solomon's."

Leaving the question of authorship, we have to ask in what sense we are to speak of these books as inspired. Are we to say, for instance, that the wisdom of the proverbs is to be an authoritative rule of conduct for us? May we quote Proverbs xiii. 24 to show that God requires every father to use the rod in educating his son, so that parents who adopt another method of training are violating a Divine precept? Are we to quote Proverbs xxii. 26 to show that God forbids us to be surety for a friend's debts? or Proverbs xxiii. 1-3 to determine the position of kings in the ideal commonwealth?

Again, are we to regard xxx. 18, 19 as a word of God, or merely a word of Agur? And to repeat a difficulty already mentioned, is xxxi. 6, 7 a precept which we are to regard as coming from the Lord of Heaven? The mere suggestion of these questions at once brings the answer. Those who are strongest in their assertion that the Bible *is* the word of God, and does not only contain it, would feel that they were demented if they answered the questions in the affirmative. It is clear that when we cite these wise utterances of Solomon as inspired, we do not mean that they are commandments of universal application. We exercise a kind of criticism; we judge them, as it were, by their own merits; we make a distinction. Some of the precepts are valuable, some are less valuable; we trace some of them in the teaching of our Blessed Lord; others we could not conceive in His lips. Thus we are driven to a historical explanation: the book contains the gnomic wisdom which was current among the inspired People; its ethical value is secondary to its historic interest; it fills a place in the development of the Divine life of the human spirit, just as the Mosaic law fills another such place; but neither the one nor the other has authority over us apart from the eternal ethical truths which are preserved, amplified, and spiritualized in the Christian code. We perceive, then, that to speak of the Proverbs of Solomon as inspired as if they were on the same plane as the precepts of the

Sermon on the Mount is a great blunder; it is to destroy all perspective; it is to reduce the Inspired Book, with its fifteen hundred years of growth and its fine sense of development, to the level of the Koran, which sprang all at once from the teaching of a single man, and is in consequence as unprogressive in its influence as it was inorganic in its origin.

The question that presents itself in connection with the inspiration of Ecclesiastes is simpler. No Christian man would dream of taking the cynical pessimism of this book with its somewhat reluctant conclusion, which treats the fear of God as the best course which can be adopted under very gloomy conditions, as a correct theory of life. The admiration which M. Rénan bestows on the book, as the most charming and only thoroughly human book in the Hebrew Bible, at once reminds us how little of the revelation of God there is in it. We may say that it finds its ideal place in the Inspired Scriptures because it is suitable that the doubting spirit, which comes to a man of many experiences and wide knowledge of the world, should find an utterance as a foil to the restful and trusting spirit which comes to a man who waits upon the Lord, and whose experience and knowledge of the world are summed up in his experience and knowledge of God. Thus the book holds a place in the Inspired Volume just because it is not, in the ordinary sense of the word, inspired itself. It stands among the books of teaching, strengthening, and consolation as Saul stands among the prophets, or as Judas among the disciples. The paragraph viii. 16–ix. 6 may be taken as an epitome of a cynical philosophy, and as such is the direct negation of all true religion; it is the denial of the possibility of revelation (viii. 17), the disbelief in the great moral Governor of the world (ix. 2–6), and consequently it reaches the impotent conclusion that the sensual joys of life are all that we are to expect (ix. 7–9), and our activity in life is to be increased by the paralyzing thought that there is no hereafter! In no part of the Bible is the danger of an ignorant employment of the phrase "word of God" more apparent. If this teaching of Ecclesiastes is "the word of God," then the radical scepticism of the Materialist is justified on the Divine authority. But we may safely say that this can only be accepted as the "word of God" at the expense of rejecting all the noblest teaching of the Law, and the Prophets, and the Gospel.

There remains the "Song of Songs." What do we mean when we say it is inspired? It owes its place in the Jewish Canon to the tradition that it was composed by Solomon. And yet what a curious contradiction is here! The Song is an epithalamium on the king's marriage with a heathen wife, and it was precisely such marriages that turned away Solomon's heart from the Lord. Respect for a great name could scarcely go further; because Solomon was counted wise,

the song which marks his entrance into folly is
held in abiding remembrance. But this is not an
exhaustive account of the matter. Whoever wrote
this poem was a poet of the highest order. It is a
lyric too luscious, too perfumed for Western taste,
but even to us surpassingly beautiful. The English
translation falls involuntarily into the exquisite lilt
of the original—

> My beloved spake, and said unto me,
> Rise up, my love, my fair one, and come away,
> For lo, the winter is past,
> The rain is over and gone;
> The flowers appear on the earth;
> The time of the singing of birds is come,
> And the voice of the turtle is heard in our land.

Or listen to the music and the roll of this—

> Who is she that looketh forth as the morning?
> Fair as the moon,
> Clear as the sun,
> Terrible as an army with banners!

If by Inspiration we meant poetic inspiration,
we should have little enough difficulty in accounting for the place of the song in an Inspired Book.
But we do not mean poetic inspiration; and of
spiritual significance or spiritual intent there is
not a trace throughout the poem. And yet if we
might give a wider meaning to the word spiritual,
we might possibly light upon a clue.

The poem is a very pure and beautiful description of a passionate love between man and woman.

Can it be that this marriage ode is meant to bring out certain ideal aspects of the marriage union which were only too little understood in the East? The love of man and wife may be, ought to be, spiritual; and even viewed from its sensuous side, as it is in the poem, it seems to contain a mystery which is deeper than appears. Nature is called in to witness the mystical wedding, because it is the very holy of holies of Nature's doings and offerings. The persistent and unexplained determination of the Jews to retain this love-song in the Canon would receive in this way a very striking explanation; it would be the claim made by God to treat the ideal marriage as a spiritual fact, and thus to prepare it to be the symbol of something more spiritual still. Thus the Jewish interpreters, having vindicated for the Song a place in their Canon, began to see in it an allegory of the relation between Jehovah and Israel; instead of the adulterous wife whom the prophets often take as the pattern of the rebellious house, a young bride utterly surrendered in her love to her beloved is made the type of the people whom the Lord loved.

When the Christian Church stepped into the place that Israel had occupied, and when the Lord constantly referred to the Kingdom of Heaven under the image of a marriage, and the apostles amplified the idea of the Church as the bride, and distinctly took the union of man and wife as the symbol of the union between Christ and His people, it is easy to see how the readers of the Old Testament in the infant Church would find in the ancient love-song an allegory; they would take the magical expressions of its poetry to give articulation to their love for their Lord and to His love for them.

Possibly the poetic inspiration in this instance lies nearer to Inspiration, as we apply the term to the Bible, than at first we saw. The poet who could sing best of the ideal marriage-love between a king and his spouse, was throwing a new ideal meaning into marriage-love and so preparing it to be the interpreter of a higher love. But if this explanation is to be admitted, we must be scrupulously careful in recognizing that the poet had no such intention himself. As little as the ordinary monarch on the throne of Israel was conscious that he was the type, or part of the type, of the King whose kingdom was to have no end, so little did the composer of this exquisite poem conceive that he was singing words which would be used, in quite a new dispensation of religious life, to express the ardent love which exists between Christ and His saints.

With this suggestion for explaining what we mean by calling the Song of Songs inspired, this chapter on the Hagiographa may fittingly find its end.

CHAPTER IX.

SUMMARY AND CONCLUSION.

This little book has been a series of hints and suggestions showing rather the lines on which we shall have to move in filling out our idea of inspiration, than the completed idea of inspiration itself. The conclusions at which in the successive chapters we have arrived must have seemed to the reader chiefly negative: we have been noting what we must not include in our idea of inspiration. But having followed out some of the points in detail, we may be able to state with a little more fulness the positive idea of inspiration to which the facts have been directing us. And indeed it is a very considerable step in the discovery of what our Inspired Book is, to get quit of the prejudices which make us try to see in it what it is not, and to make claims for it which it never makes for itself. When we have quite silenced these prejudices, then we can with an open mind, or rather we ought to say with an open heart, allow the Inspired Book to teach us itself what its inspiration is.

Hitherto we have been looking at the Bible as we might look on the reverse side of a piece of tapestry, tracing the several threads, the loose ends, the knots, the cross stitches which give us some notion of the method of its workmanship. That is the human element in the Inspired Book, and we have seen that the human element presents most of the marks of human infirmity: there are the men writing treatises for special occasions with no idea that their work is to hold a permanent place in an Inspired Volume; there are the histories growing under successive hands as histories usually do grow in an unscientific age; there are the poets singing their poems, true and beautiful poems, but by no means thinking that their compositions were to have a place in a completed whole. This human side has to be examined and understood and allowed for, otherwise we shall constantly be attributing its manifold infirmities to the Word of God, and that must always be to lay the foundations of inevitable scepticism.

Two or three conclusions may be stated with some distinctness. First of all, we may say that *the writers of the Bible are all subject to certain limitations of culture and knowledge imposed by the age in which they lived;* thus frequently the widening view of the later writer may correct the narrower view of the earlier, and even the views of the latest writers remain subject to the revision of subsequent experience; of this last observation the readiest example is the general expectation of the Apostolic age, expressed so vividly in the Revelation, that the second coming of Christ was quite near at hand. It follows, of course, that a principle of conduct, though it be prefaced by an imposing "Thus saith the Lord," is not to be taken at once as applicable to our life, authoritative as an absolute ethical law everywhere and at all times; but it must be examined in the light of after revelations and after experience; and generally, only that which is in accordance with the spirit of our Lord Jesus Christ can be ultimately accepted as valid. This is all contained germinally in our Lord's own simple statements when He drew into parallel lines of contrast what was "said to them of old time" and what He Himself says unto us.

Then, again, we may say that *historical writings in the Bible are by no means guaranteed against error;* in fact the Bible itself, by furnishing us in almost all cases with more than one account of the same transactions, implicitly warns us against the idea that they are. In this point of course our desire for certainty inclines us to demand that there should be infallibility, and our eager dogmatism therefore hastens to maintain that there is; but it is beyond question that infallibility there is not. Whatever may come of the admission, our chapters on the historical books of the New Testament and of the Old force us to admit, that the Bible histories, so far as they are histories, have to be dealt with just as we deal with other histories, subjected to the same inquiries, examined by the same principles of historical criticism. In every case, without any exception, the facts have to be discovered by the careful comparison and weighing of more or less divergent accounts.

Perhaps one other conclusion may be stated: *that the traditional authorship of the several Books of the Bible is by no means to be relied upon*, because frequently writings would cluster round the nucleus formed by a great name, and would ultimately all be treated as if they came from the one pen; thus the whole code of a highly developed law would be attributed to Moses the first founder of the Law, or the whole collection of poems in a Psalter would be ascribed to David as the earliest composer of such poems; and perhaps we may add as a further illustration, letters would be ascribed to apostles in the early Church because it was known that those particular apostles had written letters of a similar kind. But, further, there is reason to believe that the principles of literary composition, during the latter part of the period in which the Bible-books were composed, fully recognized what are called Pseudepigraphical works — that is works in which the author writes under the name of one of the great ancients, and puts his own words into his master's lips. In modern times we should be apt to call this forgery: but in ancient times what we call forgery passed as a due humility; authors were more anxious that their books should be read than that they should have the credit of writing them. The works ascribed to Solomon and Daniel in the Old Testament, and some of the Epistles which seem to be from Saint Paul in the New, may possibly be examples of this kind of literature.

This is the reverse side of the tapestry. But if we have given our attention to this side with candid and reverent minds, we shall not be the less struck with what we may call the right side, when we come to examine it. The total impression produced by the Bible on its readers is not affected —except very much for the better—by bearing in mind the conclusions arrived at. The feeling that all precepts contained in the Book are not necessarily applicable to us leads only to a closer attention and a more intelligent inquiry as to which are so applicable, leads us, in fact, to seek for the Spirit of Christ to be our interpreter. We keep vividly in our minds the evil example of the Jews, against whom our Lord brought the charge, "Ye search the scriptures, because ye think that in them ye have eternal life . . . and ye will not come to me that ye may have life" (John v. 39). We are reminded that to us as to the Jews the Scriptures may be a positive hindrance if we make them a substitute for coming to Christ; and we are content, believing that they are the witnesses of Him, to value them just in proportion as they deliver that witness, and to undervalue those parts which do not testify to Him clearly positively rejecting any part which is contrary to Him. Again, the knowledge that as historical works our Scriptures are liable to the mistakes into which human historians must always slip, throws us all the more forcibly on the spiritual significance of the narratives, and much that may have slight value as history may be rich in a kind of idealizing or allegorical teaching; until our eyes have been opened to the fallibility of the historical details, we perhaps never fully notice how little the spiritual effect of the Book depends upon these details. Again and again are the Chronicles read, and their lesson is perceived in spite of those really considerable discrepancies which we have traced between them and the parallel passages of the earlier narratives.

Then the recognition that in very many cases the authorship is doubtful, saves us from drawing erroneous conclusions which follow too easily from the traditional views of the authorship; while in the parts where we can attach no importance to the authorship, we are the more inclined to let the teaching weigh with us for what it is worth. Things which pass as the sayings of a great man have an exaggerated weight; ideas which come to us as the products of the thought of Solomon the wisest of men have the air of finality which overawes us; suffered to stand upon their own bottom they assume a less perilous pre-eminence.

At the outset we attempted to frame a provisional definition of what we must mean by inspiration. At the close it may be worth while to reconsider this definition. *We call our Bible inspired, because by reading it and studying it we can find our way to God, we can find what is His will for us and how we are to carry out His will.* How true this is ; how vain would it be, in face of all those who have found and are daily finding it true, to attempt to gainsay it. The more you consider it, the more you will see that the facts pointed out in the intervening pages since this definition was adventured, do not, and cannot, in the least affect it.

By reading and studying the Book we find our way to God. Yes surely. Howsoever it came to be what it is, whosoever actually wrote the several parts of it, it is a book which is full of God. There is no definition of Him, there is no theory about Him, but from the first page to the last it assumes Him ; it presents us with the spirit of man, coming from Him, and therefore always aspiring after Him ; it utters all the longings and the surmisings and the questionings ; all doubts and all despairs have their place here with all hopes and all certainties. Like the gradual brightening of the day, the idea of God clears as we proceed, and the way to Him gradually simplifies. Just think of this ! How obscure, for all its seeming distinctness, is the idea of the Jahve-Elohim, who walked in the Garden of Paradise and spoke to Adam, compared with the idea of the Son of God in that other garden, in intimate communion with the Father, taking the cup that was given to Him, and saying, "Thy will be done." How simple and comprehensible is this last Way to God in the Son of God become man; how living too and how energizing is this Way compared with that terrible Sinai, or even with the broken cries and the strongest utterances of the greatest of the ancient prophets.

And yet it is only the Way to God, not God Himself, that is revealed to us here. Any attempt to draw from the Book a complete conception of Him remains a failure. The Book refuses to give it; that is not its purpose; that is what the Athanasian Creed attempts to give, and with what success? No, the Bible, breathing as it does with the Spirit of God, flashing upon us the reflections of His face, now in shadowy gleams, now in startling glimpses, at length in an express image of His countenance, yet maintains its fundamental idea of God that He is invisible, incomprehensible, and quite beyond us.

By *reading and studying*, we say. And this is of the highest importance. An ingenious person has lately put together all the crude anthropomorphisms, all the childlike ideas of God as merely a larger and stronger man, which are to be gathered from hastily running through the Bible. And a very pretty picture they make. It is as if you were to run through the score of an oratorio and gather together all the flats and sharps, and play them as a specimen of the composer's skill; or as if you were to pick out all the faulty lines in the portrait of a master, and piece them together on a canvas and colour the whole with the least harmonious of the tints that had been employed. But this is not reading and studying the Bible ; it is specifically reading without studying. It is not everything said about God in the Bible, nor everything put into His lips, that is to go to form our conception of Him ; on that showing we should have to include not only the sorrowing and despairing cries of psalmists and prophets which show us that their faith sometimes failed, but also the lies which the serpent itself told about Him to Eve. It is only by studying : by patiently letting all these manifold aspirations of the heart after God, all these imperfect conceptions about Him, fall into their long series as leading up to Him who is Himself the Way to God, the Lord Jesus Christ ; only so can we find the way to God in the Bible. But so we can find it and do, as myriads now in His presence, and thousands now upon the earth, can joyfully testify.

Then we can find what is His will for us ; for us as individuals, for us as a race. We shall not find what is His will for us as individuals by finding what was His will for Noah or for Abraham, for Esau or for Jehu ; but we shall find, perhaps, by a careful study of these and the totality of instances, what was His will for the race. Let us look at this for a moment. The Old Testament presents us with the completed Law, prophetical utterances, and miscellaneous writings of the nation whose history it tells. In this completed volume we are able to detect the several strata, and so to construct with some certainty the stages by which Judaism marched from its primitive condition to its final fulfilment; we are able to mark the separation of this nation from other nations by a peculiar series of events, under the guidance of seers and legislators, of kings and prophets, and finally of priests. The impression created throughout is that this is a peculiar people, a people chosen for a special mission to the world. For more than a thousand years this people's history unfolds before our eyes, and yet it remained obscure how the Jew was to fill any important place in the human family. He had, as his books show, a constantly strengthening ethical life and a peculiarly noble poetical literature. On the other hand he tended to a narrow exclusiveness, and his religion hardened into an infinity of tedious and almost meaningless detail. Yet this religion contained a hope in its heart. It felt that all its cultus and its law were symbolical, and that the national sufferings and chastisements were pointing throughout to an unknown future which poets and prophets imperfectly foresaw. In this unique People, brought through such experiences to the social and religious and symbolical condition in which the completed Old Testament describes them, we can see written large the Will of God for the Race, for the Human Race. He had chosen Israel His servant to play a part in the religious education of man, the full meaning of which was not perceived by those who wrote, nor by those who collected, nor by those who expounded these Ancient Hebrew Scriptures. The key to it all was yet wanting; the will of God had yet to unfold itself. In the New Testament we are presented with this key, with this unfolding of the will of God. Israel as the suffering servant of God emerges into the Christ, the Son of God sent into the world to save the world. The people of Israel as a carefully organized religious community expands into a world-wide society, a veritable Kingdom of God.

But while the Bible thus shows us in broad historic sweeps the will of God for the race, in this revelation of Christ when the fulness of time should come it shows us the will of God for the individual. It is His will that each of us, through faith in the Son of God, should become a son or a daughter of God. This is the truth which forms the apex of the historic pyramid. It is, strictly speaking, only with this truth that we now in the new era are practically concerned. The wide foundations on which it is laid, the slow æonian processes by which it was reached, are all contained in the Inspired Book, and to the calm mind duly considering it, this appears the grand evidence of revelation. A human inventor of a religion would write a treatise which contains in carefully digested articles the truths and the precepts which the religion should teach: God giving to the world a religion, sets it as a tender heavenly plant in the soil of human life at the beginning, and through the long succeeding ages rears it to a slow perfection. The record of its growth thus becomes the proof of its Divine Origin. And surely no word except Inspiration can describe the book which reflects for us this wonderful process.

Then we can find out how we are to put into practice His will for us by reading and studying the Bible. How is this? Clearly there is room here for grave mistakes. The Boers of South Africa proceeded to exterminate the native races on the ground of the command which is represented as being given to the Israelites to utterly destroy the Canaanite. In the same way the organization of the Jewish people under a priestly hierarchy, and the cultus of elaborate ritual, have been taken as authoritative teaching for the Christian Church. The command given to Moses to make an altar and to offer sacrifices is treated as a command to us to make altars and to offer the sacrifice of the mass. But what limit is there to the crude perversions of the Sacred Writings which have constantly appeared and reappeared in the course of the centuries? The only way to find how we are to carry out His will for us in the present day, is to go straight to what we called just now the Apex, to that Christ who is the end of the Law to every one that believeth. It is the religion in its ultimate spiritual development, and not the more or less materialistic foreshadowings of it, with which we are concerned. When a book or a system can show us anything which is an advance on Christ Himself, then we may turn to this new development as indeed a revelation. At present Christ Himself remains quite the apex, and all the attempts to improve on Him in Churches, Councils, and Dogmas, have proved to be merely reversions to the rudiments of the world out of which in the fulness of time Christ came.

If we would put in practice God's will for us, the Bible at its highest point tells us that His will is that we should believe on Him whom He has sent; that a faith in Him constitutes a new birth, and therefore a man who is in Christ is a new creature. It tells us that Christ is with us always even unto the end of the world, and His invitation to come unto Him, learn of Him, and take His yoke, is thus valid for all times. It tells us that when by this new birth of faith we become the sons of God we receive the Spirit of God, and by the Holy Spirit are so taught that we need not "that any should teach" us. It thus presents us with a new Community gathered out of all nations, and ultimately to be drawn together in one for an eternal Assembly and Church in the Heavens, a Community which consists of those who by the new birth are in Christ, and being in Christ, are members one of another. God's will, then, declared for each of us is that, believing in His Son as our Saviour, we should become members of His Body, and pass the time of our sojourning upon the earth as becomes the children of God, in perfect love one to another, and in hourly submission to His will that He may work in us just what is well-pleasing in His sight.

The Bible at its highest point tells us this : and as the ultimate expression of the Divine purpose for human life it is surely quite obviously inspired. If proof of its inspiration were wanting, we should only have to look at the pitiful results which have ensued from leaving this ideal and attempting to fall back upon common human conceptions. We may safely say that where the Church has departed from this inspired teaching she has declined ; where she has added to it, the additions have been for the worse. Thus the ultimate truth which the Bible gives us in religion remains the ultimate truth which the world has attained. It is not by accident that the Canon closes where it does. We are in ignorance why or how the collection was so formed, leaving out what it leaves out, including only what it includes. But the controlling and ordaining wisdom of the Divine Spirit is sufficiently plain in the result. The writings, apostolic or sub-apostolic, which for a little maintained a wavering position in the collection, are writings which add nothing to the ultimate truth which we have just considered ; very quickly they begin actually to take from it and obscure it. From the end of the second century downwards—when, happily, the Inspired Book was securely marked and distinguished from other and unauthoritative writings — the decline becomes obvious and rapid. Almost all the positions which the New Testament presents as its highest and purest utterance are little by little stiffened into an illogical dogmatism, or stereotyped in misleading materialistic forms. With this sorrowful tendency of Patristic literature we are not concerned, but its main features may be mentioned.

Uninspired writings gradually blurred the inspired truth that the will of God is that we should believe on Him whom He had sent, and taught that the will of God was only that we should belong to an external organization. Uninspired writings gradually destroyed the inspired truth that faith in Christ constitutes a new birth, by maintaining that a sprinkling of water over an unconscious infant produced a new birth. Uninspired writings denied that "if any man be in Christ he is a new creature," by declaring that he is not unless he is in a particular church also. Uninspired writings unsaid the truth which the Lord Himself gave us that "where two or three are gathered in his name, He is there in the midst," maintaining that He is not there, but only in special buildings, at special altars, subject to the direction of a special priesthood. Uninspired writings made the invitation "Come unto me" inaudible, or tried to rob it of all its meaning, saying that it was only to be understood of coming to certain self-styled representatives of Him. Uninspired writings began to deny the power of the Spirit to work through whom He would and to directly teach the human spirit, declaring that only those could teach who had received imposition of bishop's hands, and only those could be taught who would accept the dogmas of man's making. Uninspired writings shattered the beautiful and ethereal idea of the Community drawn out of all nations, and consisting of those who are in Christ by faith, and substituted for it an organization with a hierarchy of priests borrowed from Judaism or from heathenism, an organization which has from time to time fallen into the most unspeakable corruptions and has always been more or less mixed up with human imperfections, and which yet, declaring that it was itself the Kingdom of God, has turned men's minds away from the real Kingdom of God which Christ came to preach.

And thus the farther we travel from the era and the contents of the Inspired Book, the more evidence do we get of its Inspiration, because the more fatal and retrogressive appear to be the divergences from it. It is a lamp to our feet indeed, and it is our own fault if we allow the lanthorn in which it is carried to hide the light, attempting to walk by uncertain reflections upon its polished surface and not by the radiance which streams from within.

If the present Inquiry has done something towards distinguishing between the lanthorn and the light, and has thus led the reader to give a more concentrated heed to the light, it has answered its purpose.

INDEX

OF BIBLICAL PASSAGES QUOTED.

GENESIS.

i-ii. 3	201
ii. 4	201
iv. 16–24	202
v.	202
vi. 13	
vii.	} 202
viii. 2 ff.	
xii. 7	48
xiii. 7	182
xiv. 14	182
xvii. 7	48
xxvi. 24	124
xxvi. 34	202
xxviii. 9	202
xxvi. 2	202

EXODUS.

xvi. 35	183
xvii. 14	196
xx.	188, 195
xx. 23–xxiii. 33	194, 197
xxiii. 14	187
xxiv. 4–7	196
xxxiv. 14-26	195, 197
xxxiv. 27	196

LEVITICUS.

xviii.	195
xviii. 25	183
xx.	195
xxiii.	188
xxv. 34	192
xxv. 39 f.	194
xxvii. 32	192

NUMBERS.

iv. 3	193
viii. 24	193
x. 11	186
xii. 3	185
xv. 32	183
xvi.	190
xviii. 21–32	192
xx. 1, 22	186
xxi. 14	184
xxi. 33	184
xxviii.	188
xxxiii.	196, 197
xxxiii. 38	186
xxxv.	192

DEUTERONOMY.

ii. 12	183
iii. 8–14	184
x. 8 f.	190
xi. 6	190
xii. 5	189
xii. 19, xiv. 27	191
xv. 12–18	194
xvi.	187
xvi. 11	191
xvii. 14–20	157
xviii. 1	190
xviii. 6	191
xxi. 5	190
xxvi. 11	191
xxvi. 12	125
xxvi. 12–15	191
xxxiii. 2	49
xxxiv. 10	7

JOSHUA.

viii. 32	196
x. 13	156
x. 33	150
xxi.	192
xxi. 43–45	150

JUDGES.

i. 29	150
x. 3	184
xviii. 29	183

1 SAMUEL.

viii.	158
ix.	158
x. 17	158
x. 25	154
xi.	158
xii.	158

1 SAMUEL (*continued*).

xiii.	158
xiv.	158
xvi.	159
xvii.	159
xvii.–xviii. 5	159
xviii. 6	159
xxi. 2	218
xxi. 19	160
xxii. 18	218
xxiii.	223
xxxi	144

2 SAMUEL.

i. 18–27	156
v. 21	145
viii. 4	145
xii. 29	145
xxiv. 1, 9, 24	146

1 KINGS.

iii. 4	147
v. 13	147
vi. 1	167
viii. 3	148
ix. 11	148
xi. 41	163
xiv. 19	163
xiv. 29	163
xvii.–xix. xxi.	165, 168
xxii.	164

2 KINGS.

x. 32	130
xiv. 25	122
xv. 30, 33	168
xvi. 2	169
xvi. 9	130
xvii. 6	131
xviii. 2	169

2 KINGS (continued).

xviii. 5	166
xxiii. 25	166

1 CHRONICLES.

iii. 19–24	143
ix. 40–44	144
x. 6	144
xiv. 12	145
xviii. 4.	145
xx. 1–3	145
xx. 5	160
xxi. 1	145
xxi. 5, 24	146
xxiii.	146
xxviii. 19	147
xxix. 29	155

2 CHRONICLES.

i. 3	147
ii. 17	148
iii. 4, 11	148
iv. 1, 5, 7	148
v. 4	148
vi. 39	148
vii. 1 f.	148
viii. 2	148
viii. 10–18	148
ix. 29	163
xi. 16	148
xiii. 9, f.	148
xiv. 5–9	148
xx. 34	144, 165
xxi. 11, f.	148
xxii. 2	148
xxiii. 2	148
xxv. 4	177
xxviii. 16	148
xxxv. 12	177

NEHEMIAH.

viii. 17	200

ESTHER.

ix. 5–17	212

BOOK OF JOB	213

PSALMS.

ii.	220, 221
vi. 5	208
viii.	220
xvi.	220
xxii.	223
xl.	220
xli.	219, 220
xlv.	220
li.	217
lii.	218
lviii. 6, 7	207
lix. 5	207
lxviii.	220
lxix.	220
lxxii	219
lxxxviii. 10	205
xcvii.	220
cii.	220
cxv. 17	208
cvi.	219
cx.	220
cxviii.	220
cxxii.	219
cl.	219

PROVERBS.

i–ix	226
x.	226
xiii. 24	227

Proverbs (continued).

xxii. 26	227
xxiii. 1–3	227
xxv–xxix.	226
xxx, xxxi.	226
xxx. 18 f.	228
xxxi. 6	15, 210, 228

Ecclesiastes.

viii. 15-ix. 6	230
ix. 2-6, 7–9	230
ix. 10	208

Solomon's Song.

. 10-12	231
vi. 10	231

Isaiah.

i. 11	218
vii. 14	105
xl.	134

Jeremiah.

xx. 7	14, 209

Book of Daniel 134

Hosea.

vi. 6	218
xi. 1	105

Amos.

i. 3–5	130
ii. 4 f.	123
ii. 6-8	122, 123
ii. 7	123
iii. 2	126
iii. 8	125

Amos (continued).

iii. 12	123
iv. 4	124, 125
v. 5	124
v. 12	122
v. 21-24	127
v. 27	124
vi. 5	123
vi. 7	124
vi. 9 f.	132
vii. 9	124
vii. 10	125
vii. 13	124
vii. 15	121
viii. 14	124
ix. 12	129, 132
ix. 15	128

Matthew.

i. 2–16	69
i. 18–ii. 1	73
i. 23	105
ii. 15	105
iv. 12	87
v. 1–12	74
viii. ix	64
x. 17	88
xv. 24	43
xvi. 18	106
xxi. 12	90
xxiii. 2	43
xxiv. 34	107
xxvi.	89
xxvi. 17	85
xxvii. 45	86
xxviii. 16–20	77

Mark.

i. 14	87

MARK (continued).

i. 40 ff.	64
xi. 15	90
xiv. 3	89
xiv. 12	85
xv. 33	86
xvi. 19	77

LUKE.

i. 1	67, 80
i. 26	73
iii. 23–38	69
v. 12–39	64
vi. 20	75
xix. 45	90
xxii. 15	85
xxiv. 50, 51	77

JOHN.

i. 35–51	89
ii. 12	87
iii. 22–30	87
v. 39	238
xvi. 2	89
xviii. 28	86
xix. 14	86
xxi. 24	91

ACTS.

iv. 25–28	222
ix. 1–19	37 f.
ix. 26–30	38
xi. 25	39
xv.	39
xvi. 6	32
xviii. 23	32
xix. 10	31
xxii. 3–16	37 f.

ACTS (continued).

xxvi. 12–19	37 f.
xxvi. 20	39

ROMANS.

iv. 2, 3	55
xv. 33	98
xvi. 1–20	98
xvi. 27	98

1 CORINTHIANS.

xv.	78

GALATIANS.

i. 12	36
i. 16	37
i. 17, 18, 19	38, 39
ii. 1–10	39
ii. 11, 12	
ii. 19	41, 42
iii. 13	41
iii. 16	48 f.
iii. 19	49
iii. 25	42
iv. 3	42
iv. 5	42
iv. 6	43
iv. 8	42
iv. 10	34, 42
iv. 13–15	33
iv. 16	34
iv. 21–31	50 f.
v. 2	42
v. 12	42
v. 16	43, 46
v. 25	43
vi. 12	42

EPHESIANS.

v. 14	104

COLOSSIANS.
ii. 16 42

2 THESSALONIANS.
ii. 1-12 107

2 TIMOTHY.
iii. 15, 16 .... 3, 12

HEBREWS, EPISTLE TO, 100

JAMES.
ii. 21 55
v. 11 215

JUDE.
14, 19 104

REVELATION.
i. 1 101
xxii. 10-12 101
xxii. 20 101

UNWIN BROTHERS, THE GRESHAM PRESS, CHILWORTH AND LONDON.

www.ingramcontent.com/pod-product-compliance
Lightning Source LLC
Chambersburg PA
CBHW031252250426
43672CB00029BA/2181